BRITAIN, FRANCE AND BELGIUM 1939-1940

Also available from Brassey's

BAYNES
The Forgotten Victor

CHARTERS & TUGWELL
Deception Operations:
Studies in the East-West Context

DANCHEV
Establishing the Anglo-American Alliance

LAFFIN
The World in Conflict 1990

SOKOLOV
Main Front

STAHLBERG
Bounden Duty

BRITAIN, FRANCE AND BELGIUM 1939-1940

Brian Bond

BRASSEY'S (UK)

Member of the Maxwell Pergamon Publishing Corporation

LONDON · OXFORD · WASHINGTON · NEW YORK · BEIJING
FRANKFURT · SÃO PAULO · SYDNEY · TOKYO · TORONTO

UK (Editorial)	Brassey's (UK) Ltd., 24 Gray's Inn Road, London WC1X 8HR, England
(Orders, all except North America)	Brassey's (UK) Ltd., Headington Hill Hall, Oxford OX3 0BW, England
USA. (Editorial)	Brassey's (US) Inc., 8000 Westpark Drive, 4th Floor, McLean, Virginia 22102, USA
(Orders, North America)	Brassey's (US) Inc., Front and Brown Streets, Riverside, New Jersey 08075, USA Tel (toll free): 800 257 5755
PEOPLE'S REPUBLIC OF CHINA	Pergamon Press, Room 4037, Qianmen Hotel, Beijing, People's Republic of China
FEDERAL REPUBLIC OF GERMANY	Pergamon Press GmbH, Hammerweg 6, D-6242 Kronberg, Federal Republic of Germany
BRAZIL	Pergamon Editora Ltda, Rua Eça de Queiros, 346, CEP 04011, Paraiso, São Paulo, Brazil
AUSTRALIA	Brassey's Australia Pty. Ltd., P.O. Box 544, Potts Point, NSW 2011, Australia
JAPAN	Pergamon Press, 5th Floor, Matsuoka Central Building, 1-7-1 Nishishinjuku, Shinjuku-ku, Tokyo 160, Japan
CANADA	Pergamon Press Canada Ltd., Suite No. 271, 253 College Street, Toronto, Ontario, Canada M5T 1R5

First edition 1975

Second edition 1990

Library of Congress Cataloging-in-Publication Data
Bond, Brian.
Britain, France and Belgium, 1939-1940/Brian Bond.
p. cm.
Rev. ed. of: France and Belgium, 1939-1940. 1975.
Includes bibliographical references.
1. World War, 1939-1945—Campaigns—Western. 2. World
War, 1939-1945—Belgium. 3. Belgium—Neutrality.
I. Bond, Brian. France and Belgium, 1939-1940. II. Title.
D756.3.B66 1990 940.54'21—dc20   89-48005

British Library Cataloguing in Publication Data
Bond, Brian, *1936-*
Britain, France and Belgium, 1939-1940.—2nd ed.
1. World War. 2. European campaigns.
I. Title II. Bond, Brian, *1936- . France and Belgium,
1939-1940.*
940.54'21

ISBN 0-08-037700-9 Hardcover

Printed in Great Britain by B.P.C.C. Wheatons Ltd., Exeter, South Devon

To the memory of my father
Edward Herbert Bond (1901-1976)

Contents

List of Maps

Acknowledgements

I should first like to thank John Barnes and the late Ronald Lewin for reading the whole book in draft at very short notice and for offering many valuable comments and criticisms, nearly all of which I have accepted. Special thanks are also due to my editors, Noble Frankland and Christopher Dowling, for their meticulous vetting of my typescript. I alone, however, am responsible for the imperfections of the book.

I am particularly indebted to Mrs A. O. Archdale, Brigadier George Davy, Lord Keyes and Colonel Roderick Macleod for generously allowing me to borrow and quote from private papers in their possession. In addition, Lord Keyes made numerous comments and criticisms of my typescript based on his great knowledge of the Belgian part in these events: I must apologize for not being able to incorporate more of Lord Keyes' suggestions into my text, and trust that his forthcoming biography of King Leopold will deal with those points on which, in his opinion, my account is inadequate or incorrect. Willoughby Pownall-Gray has kindly permitted me to draw heavily upon the diaries of Lieutenant General Sir Henry Pownall, which I have also edited for publication.

My thanks are also due to the following for allowing me to use copyright material: Lady Spears, for permission to quote from *Assignment to Catastrophe* by Major General Sir Edward Spears (Heinemann, 1954); Her Majesty's Stationery Office for permission to quote from *The History of the Second World War: The War in France and Flanders 1939-1940* (Official History) by L. F. Ellis (London, 1953); William Collins Sons & Co for permission to quote from *The Turn of the Tide 1939-1943* by Arthur Bryant (London, 1957); and Cassell & Co for permission to quote from *The Second World War* Volume II by Winston S. Churchill (London, 1949).

It is a source of great regret that my mentor, Sir Basil Liddell Hart, did not live to offer what would doubtless have been a long and critical commentary on my interpretation of a campaign about which he knew so much. Though I know he would have disputed some of my judgements, I have at least striven to maintain an impartial viewpoint—a quality which he rated very highly. Lady Liddell Hart has helped me more than she probably realizes by turning a blind eye towards my all-too-frequent raids on his incomparable library.

It is also a pleasure to have another opportunity to pay tribute to the courtesy and efficiency of the staffs of the Central and Army (Old War Office) Library and the Public Record Office.

Penultimately, and with apologies for any inadvertent omissions, the following have all helped me in a variety of ways: Lord Bridgeman, Stephen Brooks, John Cairns, Captain A. W. Clarke RN (Ret'd), Michael Dockrill, Major General L. A. Hawes, Sir Michael Howard, Lieutenant General Sir Ian Jacob, General Sir Harold Redman, Sylvia Smither and Toby Buchan.

Lastly, but in a crucial respect most important of all, I have relied entirely on my wife Madeleine to transform my untidy longhand drafts into a state fit for others' eyes. Fortunately her spelling improves as mine deteriorates.

BRIAN BOND

Author's Introduction to New Edition

THIS volume originally appeared as one of a series entitled 'The Politics and Strategy of the Second World War' edited by Drs Noble Frankland and Christopher Dowling of the Imperial War Museum. I unwisely omitted 'Britain' from the title thinking this would be self-evident. As concise, well-defined studies intended to re-examine particular campaigns in the light of existing publications and, where possible, exploit newly available documentary sources the series was generally well-received by reviewers. Unfortunately distribution of copies was poor—my own volume failed to meet a large order as a course textbook at Yale University through late delivery—and the whole series soon went out of print.

Although a great amount of scholarly work has since been published on the ill-fated operations in France 1939-1940, much of it concentrates on different aspects to those dealt with in my book which focuses on British political direction and high-level military decisions. Morover I discovered, or made first extensive use of, several documentary sources which still give the study some claims to originality. These included the Pownall Diaries (which I also edited for publication), the Macleod Papers relating to General Ironside, and the Archdale and Davy Papers. Not least important, Lord Keyes generously allowed me to make full use of his father's papers, especially the diary which Sir Roger Keyes recorded during his mission to Belgium in May 1940, and his monumental work-in-progress on the role of King Leopold III, subsequently published under the title *Outrageous Fortune* (1984) and grate-fully acknowledged in my revised text.

These documentary sources enabled me to throw new light on many aspects of what remains a controversial campaign. To give just a few examples, I showed how the British military leaders acquiesced in General Gamelin's risky and ultimately disastrous plans, only to criticize them with the wisdom of hindsight. I showed how the Mechelen incident in January 1940 greatly increased the friction in Anglo-French-Belgian relations due to inept diplomacy and Anglo-French failure to appreciate Belgium's dilemma in trying simul-taneously to secure the promise of allied military assistance while preserving her neutrality. On the British domestic front, the Pownall Diaries were invaluable in demonstrating beyond any doubt that the generals had played the leading part in bringing about the dismissal of the popular War Minister, Hore-Belisha. Pownall's and Ironside's diaries also brought out the hair-raising risks which the allies took in planning operations in Scandinavia, and how these plans adversely affected the build-up of the forces in France. Although the battle of France in May 1940 had already received exhaustive coverage, my account provided new information and new assessments of certain crucial events, such as the mis-managed Ypres conference on 21 May, the remarkably successful British action at Arras the same day, General Gort's decision to defy War Cabinet orders and retreat to the coast, and the Anglo-French muddle over provision of the rearguard and evacuation priorities at Dunkirk. Perhaps the study's greatest claim to originality lay in the extensive coverage given to the Belgian role both in the 'Phoney War' months and during the battle. Despite the efforts of Admiral Keyes and Brigadier Davy in 1940 and during the war, the importance of the Belgian role was generally not appreciated and, with a few exceptions, historians—including Churchill—and journalists had given King Leopold a bad press. While not uncritical of the King's role and of Belgian adherence to the policy of neutrality until actually invaded, I was able to show that Gort, Pownall, Brooke and other soldiers were prejudiced in this matter. Admiral Keyes's diary, for example, proved that King Leopold had given the allies ample warning of his army's impending collapse and the need to secure a ceasefire; their furious allegations of betrayal were simply unjustified.

Recent publications have obviously added to our knowledge of individuals and critical events, causing me in a few places to modify my text and in many more to amend and update my references. But I do not see any reason to change the interpretations and judgements I made on the main issues; nothing for example has appeared to undermine my opinion that Hitler did not deliberately allow the British army to escape from Dunkirk. Consequently, the text remains substantially unaltered from the original publication and has not been much expanded. However, the references have been considerably revised and updated, the bibliography expanded and illustrations added.

I am most grateful to Professor John C. Cairns for pointing out several factual errors and dubious statements, and John Lee noticed some additional mistakes. Dr Martin S. Alexander generously took time during his sabbatical to compile an extensive list of suggested additions to the bibliography. None of these friendly helpers are responsible for blemishes that remain. Lastly, I should like to thank two other old friends, Tony Trythall and Jenny Shaw of Brassey's, for making it possible to republish this study in a new edition.

January, 1990   BRIAN BOND

Introduction

The Commitment of the British Expeditionary Force to Europe before the Second World War

In the decade before the First World War a conviction grew—particularly in the Army's newly-created General Staff—that Britain's traditional interest in the Low Countries and the Channel coast would require the immediate commitment of the British Expeditionary Force to the Continent in the event of war between France and Germany. This commitment, initially strictly limited, was eventually to involve Britain in the attritional warfare of mass conscript armies on an unprecedented scale. Considering the disproportionate number of casualties to ground gained and the abominable conditions on the Western Front, the British people, civilians and soldiers alike, supported the war effort with remarkable steadfastness and docility. There were no mutinies such as occurred in the French Army, and no collapse of the command structure, as happened in Italy and Russia in the climactic year of 1917. Yet unease and doubt about the wisdom of the very commitment of British and Imperial troops to continental warfare did exist, and rapidly gathered momentum in the disappointing aftermath of a war allegedly fought 'to end wars'. The campaigns of the Somme and Passchendaele acquired symbolic overtones both of horror and futility. The reaction was all the harsher in view of the romantic illusions which hundreds of thousands of young men—ordinary working class volunteers as well as ex-public school subalterns—had gaily cherished in 1914. The considerations of 'vital strategic interests' which had shaped British policy before the war were largely forgotten in the bitter process of counting the cost. The attitude of British public opinion in the 1920s to the repetition of a conflict such as that of 1914-1918 could be summarized in two words: 'never again'.

Even in the Army, where stoic professionalism could be expected to triumph over emotional reaction to heavy losses, the immense experience gained in more than four years of Continental warfare was dissipated amazingly quickly. Whether the desire to get back to 'real soldiering' pre-1914 style owed something to a psychological need to suppress more recent nightmares as well as to 'military conservatism' is hard to discover, but there certainly

1

was a desire to put the clock back. In 1924 the Chief of the Imperial General Staff (CIGS), the Earl of Cavan, concluded a strategic survey for the Chiefs of Staff Committee by remarking: 'I maintain that under existing world conditions we require no plans of campaign (except for small wars incidental to our Imperial position)... There is no need to try to justify our existence by wasting our time and energies in the compilation of elaborate plans for wars against hypothetical enemies'. His successor, Sir George Milne, while noting in 1926 that the Army was now completely out of date, added that the war against Germany in 1914 was 'abnormal', and that although retaining fees were being paid to reservists for another Continental war it was very unlikely that they would ever be required. Two years later Milne questioned whether it was wise to specify that an Expeditionary Force should be organized with a view to a war in Afghanistan.[1] The Army appeared to be putting the clock back not merely to 1914 but to the nineteenth century, with the Russian threat to India again receiving top priority.

In fairness to the generals' tendency to revert to a 'small wars' mentality in the 1920s one must remember that Haig's great Continental Army of 1918 disappeared like snow in summer as a result first of hasty demobilization, and secondly under the blows of the Geddes Axe[2] wielded in response to the economic crisis of the early 1920s. Furthermore between 1919 and 1932 the Services languished under the Government's 'Ten Year Rule' which not only assumed for planning purposes that Britain would not be involved in a major war for the next decade, but also decreed that no Expeditionary Force need be organized.[3]

Nevertheless, despite the potent combination of a comparatively tranquil international scene, war weariness, hopes for disarmament and 'collective security', and a protracted economic crisis, Britain's military involvement in the security of Western Europe could not be entirely ignored. In addition to the Treaty of Versailles, Britain undertook further commitments to maintain the status quo of the post-war boundary settlements in Western Europe by signing the Locarno Treaty in 1925. She also maintained occupation forces in the Rhineland until 1930.

For their part the Chiefs of Staff, and in particular successive Chiefs of the Imperial General Staff, made abundantly clear the Army's deterioration year

---

[1] Cab 53/1 6th and 30th meetings of COS Committee. CAB 53/2 73rd meeting of COS.

[2] 'Geddes Axe'—named after Sir Eric Geddes whose committee recommended drastic cuts in government expenditure in 1922. The Services, along with Education, suffered particularly severely.

[3] The 'Ten Year Rule' was approved by the Cabinet in August 1919 and would therefore have expired in 1929, but in 1928, at Churchill's suggestion, it was put on a moving basis, ie the day on which serious planning for war would begin came no nearer! As the Secretary of the CID, Sir Maurice Hankey, later wryly recalled: 'When I woke up in the morning, I'd say, "Good God, the Ten Year Rule starts again this morning!"' The Rule ceased to apply only in 1933. For differing assessments of the effects of the Rule see articles in the *RUSI Journal*, March and September 1971.

by year, due mainly to the shortage of money and men. Indeed, by 1930 an Expeditionary Force for intervention in Europe could simply not be scraped together from the regular units stationed at home. As the CIGS noted in the Annual Review of Imperial Defence Policy in June 1933, 'it would be impossible for the Army to do anything serious for six months. On the outbreak of war one division or possibly two might be sent out more as a token than anything else'. Fortunately, it was felt, there was always the French Army to protect British interests against a resurgent Germany. The following year the Chiefs of Staff bluntly reported that 'so far as commitments on the Continent are concerned, the Services can only take note of them. . . ' No instructions had been given for planning should an emergency arise, consequently no detailed plans had been worked out. 'This country', they noted, 'is in a less favourable position to fulfil the Locarno guarantees than it was, without any written guarantee, to come to the assistance of France and Belgium in 1914.'[4]

While it cannot be said that any of the Army's leaders relished the prospect of preparing for a Continental commitment—but feared it might be unavoidable—some members of the National Government under MacDonald and Baldwin (1931-37) gave the impression that such an eventuality was too awful even to contemplate. Hence the following exchange in the Committee of Imperial Defence on 22 November, 1934, during a discussion of planning on a five year basis for war with Germany:

> Sir B. Eyres-Monsell (First Lord of the Admiralty) drew attention to the phrase 'Expeditionary Force' in a CID Paper. He asked whether the War Office could see their way to avoid the use of this expression, which, if used in public, would have a bad moral effect. Mr J. H. Thomas (Dominions Secretary) agreed that the expression 'Expeditionary Force' had unpleasant inferences in the public mind.
>
> The Prime Minister (Ramsay MacDonald) agreed, and asked that not only in public, but in all official papers the term 'Expeditionary Force' should not be used.[5]

Disillusionment with the results of the First World War was underlined by the flood of 'anti-war' novels and memoirs which reached its high-water mark in the late 1920s and early 1930s at the very time when the vision of a peaceful world, controlled by the League of Nations and characterized by multilateral disarmament, was beginning to fade.[6]

In Britain the anti-war reaction (not necessarily pacifist) easily merged with irritation and even outright hostility towards the recent ally but ancient

---

[4] Cab 53/4 111th and 120th meetings of COS. At the former meeting Admiral Chatfield remarked 'It had been traditional British policy never to be ready and to be rather proud of it—we must stress that this attitude is now very dangerous'.
[5] Cab 2/6 266th meeting of CID, discussing CID Paper 1149-B. The remarks quoted concerning an Expeditionary Force are of course concerned with presentation rather than principle; in fact the National Government, however reluctantly, accepted the possibility of a Continental commitment.
[6] See C. Falls *War Books: a Criticial Guide* (Peter Davies, 1930) and C. Barnett *The Collapse of British Power* (Eyre Methuen, 1972), pp. 428-35.

enemy, France. As John Cairns has written: 'The British never quite knew what to make of France: she was too weak or too strong, too independent or too obviously dependent, too much a reminder of the past, too much a warning, with her alliances, of troubles to come.'[7] Few Englishmen in the 1920s viewed with sympathy France's obsession with security vis-à-vis a disarmed and apparently reformed Germany. France's attempt to enforce the payment of reparations by invading the Ruhr in 1923 was particularly unpopular in Britain. Thus Arthur Balfour confessed in the Committee of Imperial Defence in 1924 that he found the French attitude to defence 'intolerably foolish... they are so dreadfully afraid of being swallowed up by the tiger, but yet they spend their time poking it'. Air Marshal Trenchard warned against 'tying ourselves by a pact to a country which in fifteen years is going down hill continuously, a country which is antagonistic and has piled up all this feeling against Germany.'[8] Even the late Guy Chapman, though a Francophile, expressed irritation with the French: 'Either it is *la gloire*, or *la patrie*, or *la pauvre France qui a souffert tant de peines*, or *la pauvre humanité...*' Many of those who had denounced French militarism in the 1920s inconsistently expressed their disgust at France's unwillingness to risk war with Italy in 1935.

Thereafter, in the late 1930s, France submitted to a remarkable extent to British leadership, especially with regard to Germany. Britain was not reluctant to seize the diplomatic initiative but too often in the mid-1930s seemed to exercise it at the expense of her natural ally. Churchill, who was among the minority who appreciated that Britain was ultimately dependent on a militarily strong France, exclaimed in the House of Commons on 14 March, 1934:

> The awful danger, nothing less, of our present foreign policy, is that we go on perpetually asking the French to weaken themselves... There is nothing to be said for weakening the Power on the Continent with whom you would be in alliance.[9]

One can go further and hazard the generalization that Britain's governing class was appallingly ill-informed about France and was on the whole unsympathetic to her difficulties in domestic and foreign policy. Nor of course—as was the case with Stanley Baldwin—did closer acquaintance necessarily lead to greater affection.

These considerations must be taken into account in order to understand the apparent contradiction in the attitude taken by Britain's defence experts from 1933 onwards, when the rise of Hitler followed by German rearmament at

---

[7] John C. Cairns 'Perplexities of "A Nation of Shopkeepers" in search of a suitable France, 1919-1940' in *American Historical Review*, June 1974. For a good general account of the differing French and British attitudes to European security see A. Wolfers *Britain and France between Two Wars* (New York: Norton Library Ed., 1966).

[8] Cab 2/4 195th and 196th meetings of CID.

[9] Churchill is quoted in Wolfers, *op. cit.*, p. 370, and Guy Chapman by Tairns.

last provoked a thorough reappraisal of the Continental commitment.[10] On the one hand the CID and the Chiefs of Staff maintained obstinately in the face of ministerial criticism that Britain's traditional interests on the Continent were more vital than ever (owing to the advent of air power) and that an Expeditionary Force was essential for their protection; they rejected the heresy that air power alone would decide the next war. On the other hand they consistently opposed staff talks with the French and Belgians which alone could make such a commitment practical.

Between November 1933, when the Defence Requirements Committee was set up to make a thorough survey of the deficiencies of the armed services, and 1936, the Chiefs of Staff argued through endless sub-committees that an Expeditionary Force, capable of being promptly despatched to the Continent in the event of war, must be created. The Cabinet, and in particular the Chancellor of the Exchequer, Neville Chamberlain, found this expert advice very unpalatable, but adopted a policy of masterly inactivity rather than outright rejection.

In principle a maximum of five regular divisions were to constitute the Expeditionary Force, but so long as the role remained unsettled virtually no money was made available to prepare them. War Office spokesmen repeatedly pointed out that such a small regular contingent, even if it could be placed on a war footing, made little strategic sense without a reserve, which could only be drawn from the Territorial Force. For the Cabinet as a whole this proved the sticking point—on financial perhaps more than on strategic grounds—but Neville Chamberlain also continued to challenge the strategic validity of a Continental commitment. In a typical Cabinet intervention on 16 December 1936 in opposition to the War Minister Duff Cooper, Chamberlain stressed that he was not approaching the issue from a financial standpoint:

> The doubt he felt was as to whether we were right in approaching any war from the point of view of the last war. To think we could send an Expeditionary Force at the outset of a war might involve a rude awakening... He himself doubted whether we were right in equipping the Territorial Force *for the trenches* (my emphasis). He thought the question had not been considered impartially. It was always assumed that we must make a contribution to a land war. As one of his colleagues had said, the French might not be satisfied, but it was not for the French to dictate to us the distribution of our Forces...[11]

As the debate on the role of the Army dragged on interminably into 1937

---

[10] For a concise survey see Michael Howard *The Continental Commitment* (Temple Smith, 1972), especially p. 98-117.

[11] Cab 23 75(36)3 'The Role of the British Army'. In the face of Neville Chamberlain's opposition and Baldwin's apathy, Duff Cooper (Secretary for War) could only remark in exasperation that this subject had been under discussion so long as he was a member of the Cabinet and six months before that. He was only trying to implement the original DRC recommendation (February 1934)—agreed to by all three Chiefs of Staff—that it was unsafe to send five (Regular) divisions abroad unless they could be supported within four months by four Territorial Army divisions as a minimum.

it seemed clear to the Government that the three Services could not all be rearmed on the same scale. It was not surprising that under the firm direction of Neville Chamberlain (who succeeded Baldwin as Prime Minister in May) the Army should receive the lowest priority and more especially that the continental role should be denied. By the end of the year Sir Thomas Inskip, Minister for the Co-ordination of Defence, supported by the new War Minister, Hore-Belisha, had decided that the Army's priorities must be altered to suit its reduced share of the budget. Accordingly, 'co-operation in the defence of the territories of any allies we may have in war' received the fourth and lowest priority after Imperial commitments and home defence. Inskip was clearly uneasy, as well he might be, about this change of policy, remarking that if we did have to improvise an army to go to the aid of France 'the Government of the day would most certainly be criticized for having neglected to provide against so obvious a contingency'. Curiously, in all the controversy over 'appeasement', Chamberlain's Government has received comparatively little criticism for this major error of judgement.

As a consequence of this decision the Field Force was reorganized in February 1938 with one mobile and two infantry divisions 'equipped for an Eastern theatre' (ie, the defence of Egypt) and on a lower state of preparedness for war. As Michael Howard aptly comments, 'what was generally termed a policy of "limited liability" in continental warfare had now shrunk to one of no liability at all'. Thus the advent of Britain's more active intervention in European diplomacy in pursuit of the appeasement of Nazi Germany coincided with the tacit admission that she possessed no military force capable of fighting in Europe, and was not prepared to face the financial burden of providing one. Under Chamberlain's forceful leadership Britain's policy was now clearly one of playing for time while building up her own defences.[12]

The paradox has already been noted that although Britain's military leaders favoured the creation of an Expeditionary Force, and became increasingly convinced that it would have to be used, they shunned the notion of staff talks with the French. True, staff conversations were held in 1935 as a result of the Abyssinian crisis and again the following year after the German re-occupation of the Rhineland, but these were rigorously confined to a low level of exchange of information by military attachés and consequently were of very little use. Admittedly, too, there was the diplomatic problem that Britain and France as signatories of the Locarno Treaty were not supposed to hold secret conversations without informing Germany and Italy, but this

---

[12] M. Howard, *op. cit.*, pp. 115-20. For a concise summary of the 'Role of the Army' question see Brian Bond (ed.) *Chief of Staff: the Diaries of Lieutenant General Sir Henry Pownall Vol I 1933-1940* (Leo Cooper, 1973), pp. 126-9 (henceforth referred to as *Pownall Diaries*). The paradox, that the COS wanted a Continental Army but no staff talks whereas the Foreign Office wanted staff talks but no Continental Army, is pointed out by Peter Dennis in *Decision By Default* (Routledge, 1972), pp. 117-18 *et seq.*

was transparently an excuse rather than a reason after 1935. The main objection, succinctly voiced by Major General Sir Henry Pownall, the Director of Military Operations, in February 1938 was that 'they (the French) want to get us nicely committed and tied by the leg—not merely militarily but politically as well'. In April 1938 when low level staff talks were again being arranged Pownall noted in his diary:

> We never wanted *formal* Staff Conversations, but we *do* want an interchange of information so that we can settle the administrative problems that would occur if British troops had to be landed in France. That could easily be put in hand without any sort of pledge whatever.

Sir John Slessor, Air Representative on the Joint Planning Committee in 1938, admits that the Chiefs of Staff were on weak ground in opposing conversations with the French for fear that it would precipitate German hostility. Lord Gort (CIGS 1937-9), is also criticized by his biographer for clinging to the same view during the Munich crisis of September 1938. It was all very well to talk of not being tied to the French campaign plan (about which the British knew astonishingly little), but it seemed ever more likely that if France and Germany went to war Britain would be drawn in to support the former. It was at least desirable to have an opportunity to concert strategic plans before the outbreak of war.[13]

It is hard to escape the conclusion that although the General Staff foresaw the unpleasant probability of having to fight on the Continent, they viewed the prospect of co-operating with the French with little enthusiasm. Their attitude was also inconsistent in that while they claimed that interchange of information through military attachés was adequate to co-ordinate arrangements with the French, they later protested vehemently when confined to similar contacts with neutral Belgium.

Belgium's return to a policy of strict neutrality in 1936 deserves special attention because of the influence it exerted on French and British strategic planning, not only before the outbreak of war but right through to the German invasion in May 1940. During and after that disastrous campaign there was a tendency, especially in France, to cast Belgium and her young ruler, King Leopold III, in the role of scapegoat. Recent studies have presented Belgium's agonizing dilemmas with more objectivity while effectively demolishing some long-established myths.[14]

---

[13] *Pownall Diaries* pp. 136, 143. Gort's opposition to staff talks is all the more strange in that he was willing to see the British commander-in-chief subordinated to a French generalissimo; see J. R. Colville *Man of Valour: Field Marshal Lord Gort VC* (Collins, 1972), pp. 109-10. For a graphic account of British ignorance of French war plans at the time of Munich see Sir John Slessor *The Central Blue* (Cassell, 1956), pp. 146-9.

[14] The following discussion of Belgian policy is based largely on two works: *Les Relations Militaires Franco-Belges Mars 1936-10 Mai 1940* (Centre National de la Recherche Scientifique, 1968) and D. O. Kieft *Belgium's Return to Neutrality* (Oxford, 1972).

The military agreement signed with France in 1920 had never been popular in Belgium. The most bitter opposition was only very indirectly concerned with strategic matters but derived rather from nationalistic rivalries; namely the Flemings' detestation of every aspect of French influence. Strategically, however, there was also widespread uneasiness about excessive dependence on France, hence the repeated but vain attempts to draw Britain into the agreement. The strategic doubts were on two levels, technical and political. As to the former, Belgian military opinion was, by the mid-1930s, unwilling to stake everything on a linear defence of Belgium's eastern frontiers which would in effect have constituted a continuation of the Maginot Line and would have depended on the rapid advance of French forces to reinforce the Belgian garrison. Could the Belgians stake their national existence on the immediate assistance of a condescending neighbour who in a crisis was bound to consider her own interests first? There was another snag, too. Such a strategy, in the opinion of the Belgian General Staff, would lay the country open to a German thrust through Holland and into their rear.

Reservations on grounds of policy were even more serious. Fears that the French would use Belgium as a springboard from which to launch an offensive against the Ruhr were fed by several tactless statements by French generals. In October 1930 and again in January 1933, for example, Pétain let slip that France might have to invade Belgium in order to get at Germany. Equally unpleasant was the prospect that Belgium would be drawn into war as a result of France's network of alliances in east and central Europe. The Franco-Soviet Pact of May 1935 was particularly alarming in this respect. One clause of the Franco-Belgian agreement stipulated that Belgium would mobilize if Germany did so; but would Belgium be obliged to mobilize if Germany mobilized against Poland?[15]

Thus the Belgians' desire to modify their military agreement with France was of long duration and the first step towards revision—the ending of the military alliance—was actually taken on the day before the German re-occupation of the Rhineland in March 1936. This crisis, which demonstrated that France was unwilling to fight for a crucial strategic interest of her own, and also that Britain was not prepared to make a definite military commitment to the Continent, merely strengthened Belgium's resolve to fight, if at all, solely for her own interests.

Through the summer and autumn of 1936 the Belgian Government gradually came to the conclusion that the national interest would best be served by a policy of strict neutrality: Belgium would allow her territorial integrity to be guaranteed but she would cease to be a guarantor in any treaty. Two points need to be stressed here. First, the evolution of the new policy owed little to King Leopold personally. Secondly, the main impetus behind the policy was supplied by the intense domestic rivalry between Flemings and Walloons.

---

[15] Kieft *op. cit.*, pp. 12-54 *passim. Les Relations Militaires op. cit.*, pp. 17-21.

The aim of the Van Zeeland Cabinet was first to obtain internal unity, and second to enhance Belgium's capacity to defend herself.[16]

This last point no doubt explains the initially mild reaction of Britain and France to Belgium's new policy. In July Britain declared she had no objection to the new policy, while in September the French confined their criticisms to the implications of Belgian neutrality for British intervention in event of war; namely that the RAF would lose the use of advanced bases and would be unable to fly over Belgium to bomb the Ruhr. At this time, incidentally, the French still preferred British military intervention on the Continent to be directed to Belgium.

King Leopold's harsh manner in proclaiming Belgian neutrality in October 1936 caused 'anger abroad, confusion at home and another set-back for the (Belgian) defence project'. Apart from the British Chiefs of Staff, who continued to believe that a neutral Belgium would be a more effective deterrent to Germany, Anglo-French reaction to the King's speech was at best one of irritation. The French Army in particular saw its vital strategic assumptions undermined: no longer could it hope for close co-operation with the Belgians in defending the latters' eastern borders, so ensuring that even a surprise attack by Germany would be checked beyond France's borders. Henceforth France's security would be critically dependent on the amount of military co-operation she could concert with a nominally neutral Belgium.[17]

Despite Belgium's abrogation of the military agreement with France, and despite Britain's lukewarm attitude to Anglo-French-Belgian staff talks following the re-occupation of the Rhineland, relations between the French and Belgian general staffs remained close and cordial throughout the summer of 1936. Indeed very detailed plans were agreed upon to enable the French Army to advance right up the Albert Canal in response to a German attack. Gradually, however, the King and his chief military adviser, General Raoul Van Overstraeten, an able but unpopular staff officer, took steps to bring defence arrangements into line with the new foreign policy. Defence plans were ostentatiously devised against France as well as Germany, and feelers were put out for the purchase of military materials from Britain rather than France. Above all contacts through recognized military channels (ie, general staffs and defence ministers) were broken off.

Nevertheless Belgium's position remained ambiguous. Francophobe though the attitude of the King, Van Overstraeten and the Government might appear, all were aware that they had far more cause to fear Germany than France and that, as a corollary, it would be reckless to destroy the close military rapport built up with France in recent years. A compromise policy was consequently adopted, clearly with the King's connivance, whereby information on nearly every aspect of Belgian defence policy—troop movements, communications,

---

[16] *Ibid*, pp. 56ff, 107-114. See also *Les Relations Militaires* pp. 22-7.
[17] Kieft pp. 115-48.

fixed defences, air reconnaissance arrangements etc—would be made available in the strictest secrecy to the French military attaché at Brussels. Thus the chilly demeanour with which the Belgian Government continued to reject all Anglo-French requests for staff talks—particularly in the early weeks of 1939 when a German attack on Holland was rumoured—by no means conveyed the whole story.

Indeed that there was a difference of emphasis among Belgian policy makers became evident to the British as a result of this false alarm. Whereas the King and the Foreign Office were unwilling to risk staff talks lest they became known either to the Flemings or to the Germans, the Minister of Defence (General Denis) and the Chief of the General Staff (General Van den Bergen)—though also concerned to preserve neutrality if possible—were more acutely conscious of their country's peril and attached more importance to concerting precise arrangements with Britain and France before an invasion of Holland or Belgium occurred. Thus General Van den Bergen told the British attaché that he would continue secret conversations with him and the French military attaché on his own initiative at the risk of instant dismissal if discovered.

> He would not mention such conversations to a civilian minister of National Defence (as distinct from his trusted friend General Denis) nor to the Palace group, whose optimistic and excessively neutral attitude he did not understand and thought to be rather unreal.[18]

The dilemma facing the French Commander-in-Chief, General Gamelin, remained unchanged in essentials between April 1937, when Britain and France jointly accepted Belgium's policy of neutrality and undertook to come to her aid if attacked, and the outbreak of war. Gamelin continued in vain to press for a promise that French troops would be allowed to enter Belgium before the German invasion actually occurred. Failing this arrangement, he was at pains to stress, he was unwilling to risk an encounter battle against superior forces in unprepared and unreconnoitred positions.

Gamelin's plans necessarily remained vague for want of contacts between the high commands, though it must be said that French war planning in general gave an impression of unreality. Van Overstraeten allowed select items of intelligence to filter through the Belgian general staff to Gamelin, while the latter reciprocated by passing on some confidential information, such as a new French concentration plan in September 1937. Gamelin, however, did not pose precise questions, nor did the benefits of these secret exchanges reach the lower echelons where collaboration would actually take place in event of war. In these conditions, as a colloquium of French and Belgian historians soberly concluded in 1968, no common defence could be prepared.[19]

[18] *Les Relations Militaires* pp. 30-6, 62-4. In February 1938 Van den Bergen appears to have acted on his own initiative in presenting the British with a map showing Belgian military dispositions. See Kieft, p. 161, n2.
[19] *Ibid*, pp. 38-42 and 59 (text of Anglo-French Declaration, 24 April 1937).

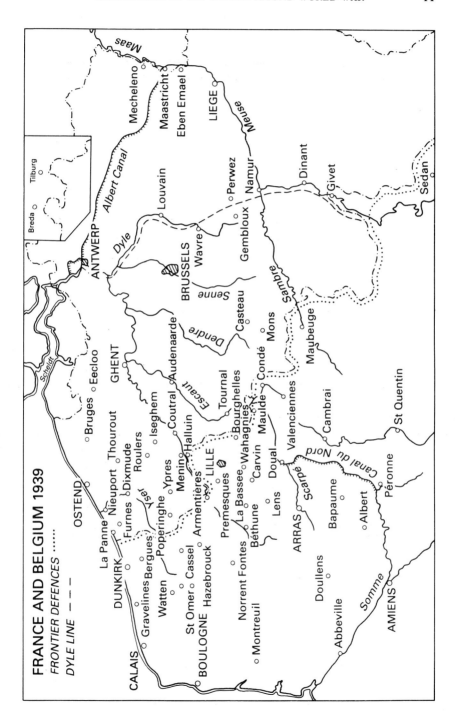

FRANCE AND BELGIUM 1939
FRONTIER DEFENCES ······
DYLE LINE – – –

The Munich settlement of September 1938, which removed thirty-five well-equipped Czech divisions from the balance of forces opposed to Germany and shattered the credibility of France's alliance system in central and eastern Europe, should have revealed immediately the fatuity of Britain's policy of limited liability. Curiously the Chiefs of Staff in their consistently pessimistic reports on the possibility of successful support of Czechoslovakia, paid little attention to the demoralizing effects that the loss of the latter's armed forces and munitions industry would have on the French. Nor was the British Government quick to grasp the military logic of its appeasement diplomacy.[20] In short, if the case for limited liability had been dubious before Munich, it became quite untenable as a result of the strategic trans-formation effected there.

The gradual swing towards acceptance of a Continental commitment can be plotted from the minutes of CID meetings. On 15 September, 1938 Sir Kingsley Wood (Secretary for Air) could assert without contradiction that 'the first duty of the Army was the defence of this country, and this task had a priority higher than the provision of an Expeditionary Force'; while the Treasury view, according to Sir Warren Fisher, was that 'a winter campaign on the Continent in the near future was an extremely unlikely contingency'. By 15 December Lord Halifax (Foreign Secretary) was becoming uneasy about French morale, though he had recently been obliged to tell them that 'as we did not possess a field army which was fully equipped for war at the present time, further discussion of such assistance would be academic... A time might come', he warned, 'When the French would cease to be enthusiastic about their relations with Great Britain if they were left with the impression that it was they who must bear the brunt of the fighting and slaughter on land'. A flood of reports from the British ambassador and military attaché in Paris at the turn of the year left no doubt that that time had already come. The French General Staff looked to Britain to provide the divisions lost to the alliance in Central Europe; while French public opinion was ominously demanding from Britain 'un effort du sang'.[21] By 26 January, 1939 the writing was on the wall for Hore-Belisha, and likewise for Halifax. The latter candidly admitted that 'for a long time he had tried to think that a war of limited liability was possible but he was now convinced that we must abandon such a conception'.[22] Other members of the Government, notably the Prime Minister and the Chancellor of the Exchequer (Sir John Simon), were slower to yield, but on 22 February the Cabinet agreed that in the

[20] M. Howard, *op. cit.*, p. 125. For a favourable view on Czechoslovakia's prospects of defending herself against Germany, see David Vital 'Czecho-Slovakia and the Powers, September 1938' in *Journal of Contemporary History* Vol I, No. 4, 1966, pp. 37-67.

[21] Cab 2/8 332nd and 341st meetings of CID. Sir Samuel Hoare (Home Secretary) replied revealingly to Lord Halifax 'Whatever the French might think, their interests were so bound up with ours that they could not afford to stand aloof' (in the event of German hostility being directed at Britain).

[22] *Ibid* 345th meeting of CID.

forthcoming staff conversations with France we should promise to send the first two Regular divisions to the Continent in the event of war. No similar undertaking, however, was to be given regarding the Territorial Army.[23]

Although hopes of appeasing Germany died slowly and were not destroyed at Munich, Hitler's annexation of the non-German territories of Czechoslovakia on 15 March, 1939 forced the British Government to face the harsh reality that war was probably unavoidable. In the next six weeks 'limited liability' was abandoned with a vengeance and steps were taken—often without consulting the military experts—which had been regarded as unthinkable only a few months before. At the end of March the Prime Minister and the Secretary of State for War decided, almost casually, to double the size of the Territorial Army from thirteen to twenty-six divisions without even consulting the Chiefs of Staff. A guarantee was given to Poland as a warning gesture to Hitler, though how it was to be implemented militarily if the bluff was called was scarcely considered. In April a more definite commitment to send an Expeditionary Force to France was entered into than had existed before 1914; and before that month was out a measure of compulsory military training had been introduced—mainly to impress the new spirit of determined resistance to aggression on the French. On the whole these emergency actions met with public approval. Even the General Staff accepted the doubling of the Territorial Army and conscription philosophically: true, in the short term these measures would actually reduce the Army's efficiency but at least the most chaotic period might be muddled through before the outbreak of war.[24]

The belated acceptance of a Continental commitment made full staff conversations with the French both possible and necessary. At the first meeting, on 29 March, 1939, the French delegation stressed that France's first objective in a war with Germany would be the defence of her own territory. The allies would have to concentrate all their energies initially on stopping an enemy who would have superiority on land and in the air but would be inferior at sea and in general economic strength. Thus, apart from a vigorous economic blockade, allied strategy must at first be essentially defensive. Admittedly the French then contemplated a prompt counter-offensive against Italy, but as the summer wore on it seemed increasingly probable that Italy would remain neutral at first, and it was agreed that on balance it was in our interests to keep her so.[25] As regards Poland, the Anglo-French military experts felt obliged to take a somewhat cynical view. Assuming (correctly) that Hitler would first attack eastward, Poland would be valuable to the allies in providing a second front, but 'her fate would depend upon the ultimate outcome of the war'. On the whole the military experts appreciated the strategic value of a Russian alliance better than the

---

[23] Cab 23 8(39) 22 February 1939. 'Preparedness of the Army in relation to its Rôle'.
[24] *Pownall Diaries* pp. 188-201. M. Howard, *op. cit.*, pp. 128-30.
[25] See R. Macleod and D. Kelly (eds) *The Ironside Diaries 1937-1940* (henceforth referred to as *Ironside Diaries*) (Constable, 1962), pp. 75-85 *passim* for Ironside's preference for attacking Italy.

politicians, but once Poland had been guaranteed it was always doubtful if such an alliance were obtainable since the Western Powers were asking so much and offering so little.

The Anglo-French staffs were also agreed that in view of the defensive strength of the Maginot Line the Germans would probably attempt to repeat the wheeling manoeuvre of 1914, but extended further to the north and powerfully reinforced by armoured fighting vehicles and air forces. Here was Gamelin's vision of the opening German move:

> Covering their flank in Belgian Luxembourg and immobilizing the defences of the French fortified position east of Montmédy with as few forces as is possible, the Germans would launch the main body of their troops from the front Cleves-Duren on the axis Brussels-Cambrai with the object of reaching the French position from Hirson to the North Sea by overwhelming the Belgian and Dutch defences.

There seemed to be little hope of providing effective support to Holland against an *attaque brusquée*, but the French were confident of holding a line somewhere in Belgium, not forgetting that that country provided the most favourable jumping-off ground for an eventual counter-offensive.[26]

In view of the small scale of Britain's initial Expeditionary Force it was unavoidable that in the main Britain would have to conform to French wishes as regards both strategy and command system, but in any case the then CIGS, Lord Gort, was determined that there should be no repetition of the friction that characterized Anglo-French military relations in the First World War, and in which an Allied Supreme Commander was not appointed until the Spring of 1918. To be sure the British Expeditionary Force could hardly claim an independent role since it would at first comprise only two corps of two divisions each, to be despatched to France within thirty-three days of mobilization. It was agreed that the first two corps of the BEF would assemble at Picquigny on the Somme, and would later move up to the Belgian frontier on the left of the French 1 Army.[27]

This force contained forty-three infantry battalions but only one army tank battalion and two regiments of light tanks—the first armoured division would not be ready to take the field until about eight months after the outbreak of war. The BEF would also control its own air component, comprising two bomber reconnaissance squadrons, six army co-operation squadrons and four fighter squadrons. The Advanced Air Striking Force of

[26] Cab 53/49. 914 'Anglo-French Staff Conversations 1939'. L. F. Ellis *The War in France and Flanders 1939-1940* (HMSO, 1953), pp. 3-5. J. R. M. Butler *Grand Strategy* Vol II (HMSO, 1957), pp. 11-15.

[27] According to Brigadier L. A. Hawes the first Anglo-French staff conversations held in France in 1939 were completely one-sided. 'There were no interpreters present and General Gamelin spoke so quickly that I am quite sure half of what he said was not understood by the British... General Gamelin would talk at great length very rapidly for some minutes about the various proposals and General Gort would reply at once: "D'accord".' 'The Story of the "W" Plan: the move of our forces to France in 1939' in *The Army Quarterly* July 1971, pp. 445-56.

medium bombers, though stationed in France, was given an independent bombing role and remained under the direction of the Air Staff.

In the course of the summer it was agreed that the higher direction of strategy should be placed in the hands of a Supreme War Council composed of the Prime Minister and one other Minister from each country and advised by the Chiefs of Staff. The Field Force would come under the 'Command of the French Commander-in-Chief North East Theatre of Operations' (General Georges), but its Commander retained the right to appeal to the British Government if any order given by the French general appeared to imperil his force. Thus, as the Director of Military Operations noted on 3 July:

> We shall get unity of command in the field from the outset, instead of wasting three and a half years trying to get there. It may be a bold step but I'm sure it's right. Independent commands like that of Sir John French (1914-15) are all very well when times are good, fair or indifferent. But when times are bad they are most dangerous.[28]

Even before the doubling of the Territorial Army and the introduction of compulsory military training, the Regular Army was utterly unprepared for war owing primarily to the long controversy over its role and the priority given to home defence and to the other Services. It is no exaggeration to say that an Expeditionary Force of two (and later four) divisions had to be improvised virtually from scratch between April and August 1939. For example, General Ironside, the GOC Eastern District, was appalled to discover that Britain was only capable of putting two divisions in the field, and even these would be lacking in certain types of specialist troops and short of essential equipment. He added that the German military attaché attending our manoeuvres would not believe that we had not many new weapons concealed in stores which we did not intend to show until the moment came!

Although the General Staff at the War Office had, since 1933, consistently advocated a Continental role for the Field Force, Ironside and some other senior officers commanding troops felt that the position was so hopeless that a policy of limited liability was the only role which made sense. Thus, as late as 29 May, 1938, Ironside could write 'Never again shall we even contemplate a Force for a foreign country. Our contribution is to be the Navy and the RAF'. Despite brilliant last-minute improvisation, the first four divisions of the BEF sailed to France in September seriously short of munitions and every type of equipment, especially guns and tanks, while the army at home was reduced to 'a token force of semi-trained troops' lacking the equipment with which to train. In August a War Office spokesman admitted that there were at present sixty infantry tanks, against a total requirement of 1,646. It was fortunate that the BEF was given the respite of the 'Phoney War'; indeed, as Michael Howard has remarked, even Dunkirk was a mercy in that it enabled the bulk of the British Army to expand and train at leisure.[29]

[28] *Pownall Diaries* pp. 211-13. Colville, *op. cit.*, pp. 125-6. Ellis pp. 6-7, 11-12.
[29] *Ironside Diaries* pp. 51-60 *passim*. See also Butler pp. 27-9, and M. Howard p. 130.

It is also as well to emphasize the obvious but easily overlooked point that without detailed administrative arrangements even the most brilliant operational plans are worthless. That the BEF's mobilization, transportation to its allotted French ports and advance to its assembly areas all went comparatively smoothly was primarily due to a year's painstaking staff work and liaison by Brigadier L. A. Hawes and a small team of officers at the War Office.[30]

When Brigadier Hawes took up his appointment in mid-1938 he found nothing in the form of a worthwhile plan even for the scanty force then available. There was no accurate information about conditions in France, particularly as regards ports and railways. For example, a statement of the number of quays and docks available was useless without mention of the depth of water and navigational hazards. Worse still, there were no up-to-date maps of France available. There were so few administrative personnel available from the RAOC, RASC, Royal Engineers and Royal Signals that at the time of the Munich crisis it would have been practically impossible for the Army to mobilize: for one thing the only mobilization tables available were for horse-drawn units. In fact, Hawes sums up, when war appeared imminent in late August 1938 the War Office 'was like an ant heap that had been stirred up with a stick'.

After gathering as much information from the French as possible by an exchange of questionnaires, Hawes and his subordinates paid several visits to the main ports which would be used by the BEF, including Nantes, St Nazaire, Brest and Havre, and they also arranged billeting for a vast headquarters in the concentration area.[31]

The main points of the Army plan (W4) were as follows:

1. Because of the risk of air attack the main ports of disembarkation in France were to be on the western coast. This meant a longer sea passage, but was thought to be safer than the use of the Channel ports both for shipping and for the landing of troops, equipment, supplies and stores.
2. There were to be two main bases—a northern base at Rennes and a southern base at St Nazaire-Nantes. There was also to be a medical base at Dieppe.
3. The chief ports to be used were Cherbourg (for personnel, with motor transport and drivers); Brest (all stores for the northern base, with motor transport and drivers); St Nazaire (ammunition and frozen meat for the southern base, with motor transport and drivers); and Nantes (other stores for the southern base and, again, motor transport and drivers).[32]

By July 1939 maps had arrived, the naval escort had been arranged and planning was nearly complete. The last major peacetime achievement of the administrative planners was to mislead the Germans as to which ports the British would use. Dummy reconnaissances persuaded the enemy to concentrate

---

[30] The following paragraphs on the administrative arrangements for the Field Force are based on Major General L. A. Hawes' article cited in Note 27 above.
[31] Ironside was under the false impression that GHQ staff was smaller than in 1914 (*Ironside Diaries* p. 79), but Hawes, *op. cit.*, p. 454 shows that initially it was enormous—no fewer than 259 staff officers to control two divisions!
[32] Ellis pp. 9-10.

his submarines on the Havre-Rouen-Dieppe area to the neglect of Nantes-St Nazaire. Until 15 August arrangements existed for the despatch of only two divisions but they were expanded to cover four just before the outbreak of war. The Directors of the War Office Departments were only handed the detailed plans at the last moment and the planners retired to the background.

In the hasty discussions following the acceptance of a Continental role for the Field Force, the British Government paid considerable attention to the higher control of Anglo-French strategy but curiously little to a choice of commander for the Force. Lord Gort's biographer attributes this omission, surely correctly, to the fact that 'the ruling cabal was utterly divorced, in interest and experience, from military affairs. The command would be of vital interest to the nation: yet, subject to the Cabinet's final endorsement, Chamberlain was content to leave the decision to the Secretary of State for War.'[33] The most obvious disadvantage resulting from this omission was that the staff officers and unit commanders could not train under their chief's direction and build up a team spirit before the outbreak of war. Even more seriously, the last-minute selection resulted in some questionable appointments whose repercussions were apparent throughout the campaign in France.

In May 1939 Hore-Belisha consulted his *éminence grise, The Times'* military correspondent, Captain B. H. Liddell Hart, as to the relative abilities of Alexander, Maitland Wilson, Dill, Wavell and Ironside as potential Cs-in-C. Liddell Hart, characteristically, plumped for two dynamic outsiders in Hobart and Pile—who were both advocates of tank warfare—and also spoke highly of Adam, then Deputy CIGS at the War Office (and really the mainstay of the General Staff, since Gort was scarcely on speaking terms with Hore-Belisha). The latter, however, announced that he intended to recall Ironside from Gibralter with the title of Inspector-General of the Overseas Forces as potential C-in-C of the Field Force if war came.

Ironside thus returned to England with the conviction that he was to command the Field Force. A French staff officer had already told Gamelin on 8 June that Ironside would be easy to work with, and after a conversation with Gort on 1 July Ironside noted that the only thing he had found out was that the main reason for his coming home was to command the BEF in case of war. Hore-Belisha encouraged him in this belief, which was further strengthened by the fact that Sir John French had briefly had a similar post before being appointed to command the BEF in 1914. Another strong contender for the appointment was Sir John Dill, who was then GOC-in-C Southern Command. Senior French officers, including Gamelin, who attended the Aldershot Tattoo in June certainly left with the impression that Dill was commander-in-chief designate and made it plain that he would be very acceptable to them. Yet during this same French visit, General Lelong, their military attaché, mentioned to Brigadier Beaumont Nesbitt, formerly British

[33] Colville p. 134.

military attaché in Paris and now back at the War Office, that Gort would be very acceptable to the French as commander of the Field Force whereas Ironside would not. Whether this opinion filtered through to Hore-Belisha and if so how much it influenced him is uncertain.[34]

The awkward situation that prevailed in the three months before the outbreak of war can be summarized as follows: the responsibilities of Ironside and Gort were not clearly distinguished and the former had good reason to believe that he would command the Field Force; Dill's experience and present command also gave him a strong lien on the appointment; Gort's relations with Hore-Belisha were so strained that he was eager to quit the War Office and knew the minister would be relieved to see him go.

Hore-Belisha's failure to reach a firm decision led to a tragi-comic episode on the outbreak of war on 3 September 1939. Ironside, reasonably assuming that he would be appointed, sent his chief staff officer, Colonel Roderick Macleod, to Aldershot to organize his GHQ staff, but then hung about vainly awaiting a call from the War Office. According to P. J. Grigg, the forceful Permanent Under-Secretary of State, Hore-Belisha was still set on making Ironside CIGS or C-in-C, but Grigg urged that he should be given neither and that the best combination would be Gort as C-in-C and Dill as CIGS. Hore-Belisha, however, accepted only the former recommendation, and won over his fellow Service ministers and the new War Cabinet to Gort's appointment. According to Liddell Hart 'Gort was eager to take the field as C-in-C of the BEF, so Hore-Belisha and the Cabinet met his wish', but there is no other evidence that the initiative came from Gort, though he was certainly delighted. Hore-Belisha's proposal of Ironside as CIGS met with some opposition from the War Cabinet on the grounds of his lack of judgement and discretion, but Churchill's strong backing was decisive.

Ironside has described the dramatic scene at the War Office in which Hore-Belisha first persuaded him, by an appeal to soldierly duty, to accept the uncongenial post of CIGS, and then ushered in Gort from his private office with the words 'And here is the Commander-in-Chief'. Gort at once asked for Pownall (the Director of Military Operations) as his Chief of Staff, and got his way despite Ironside's reasonable objection that this would deprive the War Office of the two men chiefly responsible for military planning and liaison with the French, and so repeat the mistake of 1914.[35]

Of these appointments, Ironside's was the most questionable. He had had more experience of senior command in war than any other serving British general, but had no experience whatever of staff work at the War Office, and was by his own admission in his diaries unsuited to be CIGS. Whether he would have done better than Gort is impossible to say; he might conceivably

---

[34] B. H. Liddell Hart Memoirs (Cassell, 1965) II, pp. 238-9. Colville p. 129. Ironside Diaries pp. 76, 79.
[35] Liddell Hart Memoirs II p. 261. R. J. Minney The Private Papers of Hore-Belisha (Collins, 1960), pp. 229-30. Ironside Diaries pp. 93-4. Pownall Diaries pp. 223-4.

have been less subservient in accepting French strategic planning during the Phoney War, and he would surely have taken a stronger independent line during the early stages of the operations in May 1940. Dill was better suited in terms of physical fitness and ability to be CIGS than a Corps commander and he certainly proved better at the job than Ironside, whom he replaced in May 1940. Gort at least did well to quit the War Office, not only because of his exceedingly poor relationship with Hore-Belisha, but also because—in the admirably impartial summing up of his biographer—'he would have been far out of his depth as CIGS under Churchill's wartime Government'. Despite his Irish blood, Gort was English to the core: 'the kind of Englishman who, while accepting genuine foreigners as a regrettable necessity, finds foreign touches and tendencies in a compatriot wholly repellent'. In his relationship with Hore-Belisha, 'Gort stood too firmly by his principles and it cannot be denied that he sometimes confused principle and prejudice'.[36] It would be premature here to offer any verdict on Gort's performance as C-in-C of the BEF, but it should be mentioned that his personal position was a delicate one. His two corps commanders, Dill and Brooke, had both been senior to him in the Army List; the former had been twice passed over in Gort's favour (first as CIGS and now as C-in-C) while the latter was a highly intelligent officer to whom diplomatic tact and moderation in judgement did not come easily. Finally, all three were Irishmen.

Four points need to be emphasized in summing up this introductory chapter, all of which were to play significant parts in the drama which culminated in the collapse of France and the expulsion of the British army from the Continent.

First, the British Government's prevarication and patent reluctance in accepting a Continental military commitment was found to have serious political and military repercussions. Politically it convinced many sections of French opinion that *Albion perfide* was once again preparing to fight to the last Frenchman. The French Army's arrogance was scarcely reduced by the belated and token contribution from Britain. Moreover, although Belgium's adoption of a policy of neutrality was primarily inspired by domestic issues, Britain's failure to supply a military counterweight to French influence also played a significant part. King Leopold and his principal advisers made no secret of the fact, both before and during the period of hostilities, that they preferred to lean on British rather than French assistance. Militarily, the crucial years of indecision as to the Army's most likely tasks in war meant that even when, in 1936, a policy of rearmament was definitely accepted the Army failed to derive anywhere near full benefit from it. Thus the outbreak of war found the Army struggling, like Sisyphus, with enormous problems of manpower and equipment which could hardly be surmounted, even in the most favourable circumstances, before 1942.

[36] Colville pp. 137-8, 145.

Secondly, Anglo-French contingency planning in the summer of 1939 was badly adapted to meet the political and strategic situation that arose in September. Underestimating the power and skill of the German *blitzkrieg*, the Anglo-French defensive posture on land offered virtually no support to Poland in her hour of need. Indeed the Allies' failure to achieve any agreement with the Soviet Union rendered them impotent in eastern Europe and the Balkans, and at the same time blunted the edge of economic pressure on Germany. Italy's decision to remain neutral had some advantages, but it also deprived the Allies of their one opportunity for an early successful offensive. Whereas the decisive possibilities of *blitzkrieg* had been underestimated, Germany's capacity (and intention) to launch an aerial *blitzkrieg* on Paris and London was overestimated. Consequently the Allies' other offensive instrument of strategic bombing was not used at the outset of the war for fear of devastating retaliation.

Thirdly, Belgium's return to a policy of strict neutrality, though understandable from her own viewpoint and actually applauded at first by the Chiefs of Staff, led to much ill-will and resentment in France; while even in Britain ugly rumours circulated that the King of the Belgians and his chief military adviser were pro-German. Gamelin's dilemma of how to check a German attack well forward in Belgium without prior joint-planning and in the knowledge that he would only be invited in after the attack had begun, was to constitute his most difficult strategic problem throughout the Phoney War.

Finally, in the sphere of grand strategy, Britain and France had pursued markedly different foreign and defence policies throughout the inter-war period; above all on the problem of how strong Germany could be permitted to become without menacing the vital interests of the two countries. Nor had these differences been modified to any appreciable extent by nostalgic memories of the Entente Cordiale and the common sacrifices of the Great War. Britain and France went to war superficially united by the urgent short-term need to stop German military expansion, but there was no accord on deeper issues of national interests and grand strategy. Indeed, such delicate matters were scarcely discussed during the few months of the alliance's wartime existence. Potentially divisive issues were suppressed at first because of apprehension about an imminent German onslaught against Western Europe, and later postponed by a complacent belief that Hitler had 'missed the bus' and lost the opportunity to win a short war. The catastrophe of May 1940 cruelly exposed these deep underlying differences between the Allies, creating misunderstandings and resentments which are unlikely to be healed for at least another generation.[37]

---

[37] Eleanor M. Gates *End of the Affair: the Collapse of the Anglo-French Alliance 1939-1940* (Allen & Unwin, 1981).

1

Anglo-French Strategy and the Problem of Belgian Neutrality
September-December 1939

As explained in the introductory chapter, the difficulties posed by Belgium's neutrality were far from new for Anglo-French strategists on the outbreak of war, since Belgium had made her position abundantly clear from the autumn of 1936. Contrary to what was formerly believed, Belgium continued to supply military intelligence to Britain and France in secret and received a certain amount in return. Nevertheless the Belgian problem plagued the Allies throughout the 'Phoney War' period; exerted a decisive influence on the operational plan eventually adopted; and critically affected the outcome of the campaign in May 1940. At the time, and in the bitter aftermath of defeat, it was all too easy to make a whipping boy of the Belgians—and especially their king, Leopold III—but at this distance in time, and with fuller documentary evidence available, it should be possible to be more objective.

When the policy of military isolationism was abandoned by the British Cabinet in February 1939, Belgium was invited to join in staff conversations on a wider scale than those formerly contemplated, but declined; consequently no approach was made to the Netherlands. Thus the Anglo-French dilemma was posed: if Belgium was attacked by Germany she would probably appeal for Allied help, but the effectiveness of that help would depend largely on the Allies being previously taken into her confidence as to her military plans and defences.[1]

This problem was examined in a joint Anglo-French staff paper dated 2nd May 1939. The duration of Belgian and Dutch resistance would of course depend initially on their own preparations and speedy mobilization, but also—for anything beyond a few days—on the support of French and British

---

[1] J. R. M. Butler *Grand Strategy* Vol. II, *op. cit.*, pp. 157-8.

forces. There was little hope of reinforcing the Dutch on land, but prospects in Belgium seemed brighter provided the Allies were given detailed information in advance and were immediately invited to intervene by the Belgian Government in the event of attack.

The Allied preoccupation, then and later, was to avoid an encounter battle against superior forces in unprepared positions and with inadequate reserves. The choice appeared to lie between reinforcing the Belgians on their eastern frontier (the Meuse-Albert Canal line) and holding the Scheldt on the line Tournai-Audenaarde, thus linking the French frontier defences at Maulde with the Belgian 'National Redoubt' covering Ghent and Antwerp. No prepared defensive line as yet existed in between. In the absence of full staff conversations it seemed probable that the Allies would not venture initially beyond the Scheldt even though, military weakness apart, this had the unpalatable political implication that most of the Belgian homeland would be abandoned to the enemy. Militarily the Scheldt line would give the Allies an extremely cramped rear area almost at right angles to the French frontier defences; while for the British their line of communications to their principal bases in the Biscay ports would be parallel with their front. Despite these drawbacks plans for an advance to the Scheldt, or to the Dyle if circumstances were propitious, were approved by General Gamelin and remained the agreed Allied strategy when war broke out.

The Chiefs of Staff had always made it clear that in terms of direct military assistance there was very little Britain and France could do in a short war in fulfilment of their guarantee to Poland. In theory, however, a strong case could be made for indirect support in the form of strategic bombing coupled with an all-out attack on the Western Front in September or early October, while the German defenders in the Siegfried line were considerably inferior in numbers to the French opposite them. There has been no lack of historians such as Jon Kimche (*The Unfought Battle*, 1968) to argue this hypothesis, but we need only note the fact that Gamelin had no intention whatever of launching such an offensive until the French Army was fully mobilized— a matter of several months at least—and that his cautious attitude was endorsed by the French Government. Since Britain had as yet virtually no Army in the field she was in no position to upbraid her ally, but in any case there was little inclination to do so. The British Government was equally circumspect in the one offensive avenue open to it; namely the bombing of the Ruhr.

Sir John Slessor has recorded a vivid description of the Chiefs of Staff's first visit to Gamelin's Supreme Headquarters on 5 September. Shut away in the fortress of Vinçennes, the command post was far too cloistered and remote; a little army 'brains trust' inadequately staffed and out of touch with day-to-day developments. Gamelin described his plan for a methodical mobilization and slow advance to the Maginot Line, whence the French would proceed to 'lean against the Siegfried Line'. He had no intention of rushing the operations and risking the loss of the flower of the French Army by precipitate action. He also spoke of a limited offensive on the Saar front, but it was evidently to be little more than a gesture. Slessor got the impression that he expected very little of it, but it was something—one could not sit back and do nothing while ' *les pauvres Polonais*' were having hell knocked out of them. Slessor's summing up of Gamelin was devastating: 'a nice old gentleman, not remotely equal to his enormous job'.[2]

Ironside, the CIGS, noted that the French hoped to be facing the Siegfried Line by 17 September. Gamelin intended to bring up his heavy artillery and carry out a cautious preparatory bombardment to test the strength of the German defences. A week later, at the first meeting of the Supreme War Council at Abbeville, Gamelin repeated that he was confining his activities to no-man's-land and had no intention of throwing his army against the German main defences. Neville Chamberlain endorsed this strategy, adding that Britain was preparing for a three years' war. While Churchill thought it would be a good thing if the Germans did attempt a strong attack in the West, the prevalent attitude, repeated on numerous occasions by the Prime Minister, Chatfield, Daladier and others, was that time was on the Allied side: if only they could hold out until next spring the German prospects of a successful attack in the West would be slim. As Oliver Harvey—reflecting generally on Britain's prospects in a protracted war—confided to his diary on 22 September: 'If Germany cannot win a quick success, she cannot hope to win a long drawn war. Our problem is to hold up and contain early German onslaughts while our long term weapons come into play and the German population and German resources are worn down. The role of our army, navy and air force must therefore be essentially defensive'.[3]

With the wisdom of hindsight it is tempting to ridicule this complacency but, excepting the failure to appreciate the revolutionary nature of the *blitzkrieg* against Poland or to understand the total, binding hold which the Führer exerted over the German people, a Fabian strategy was not so unreasonable in September 1939.

It was consistent with this cautious, long-term strategy that British professional military opinion at the outset of the war should be strongly opposed to any advance into Belgium. The CIGS's diary for September 1939 contains numerous entries on the folly of allowing the BEF to advance into Belgium, though Ironside did not believe the Germans would attack until the following spring; and on the 16th he noted that the King was writing to Leopold to tell him that if there was no time to reconnoitre it might not be possible to help Belgium. On 19 September Ironside told the Cabinet that Gamelin

[2] Slessor *The Central Blue op. cit.*, pp. 242-4.
[3] Cab 65/3 War Cabinet Confidential Annexes WM4(39)1, 5 September and 16(39)7, 15 September. Cab 66/1 War Cabinet Memoranda WP(39)38, 12 September. Macleod and Kelly (eds) *The Ironside Diaries 1937-1940 op. cit.*, pp. 101-2. J. Harvey (ed) *The Diplomatic Diaries of Oliver Harvey 1937-1940* (Collins, 1970) p. 321.

feared an imminent attack through the Low Countries, but he advised emphatically that unless the Belgians co-operated at once the British should not contemplate moving into Belgium to help them at a future date. The previous day the Chiefs of Staff Committee had reached the same conclusion in an appreciation of 'The Possible Future Course of the War'.

If the Belgians would co-operate in advance, said the Chiefs of Staff, it might be possible to hold the line Givet-Namur or, failing that, the Scheldt from Audenaarde to Ghent, but otherwise the British must press the French to agree to meet an attack on the Franco-Belgian frontier. They also pointed out that the RAF would have to bomb German columns as soon as possible and this would unavoidably involve Dutch and Belgian towns. In a subsequent War Cabinet meeting on 27 September, the CIGS voiced his apprehension that Lord Gort might be ordered by the French Commander-in-Chief to advance into Belgium and face another Mons: he would then (like his predecessor, Sir John French, in August 1914) have to exercise his right of appeal to the Cabinet.

The Secretary of State for War had gathered from conversations with Daladier and Gamelin that the French would on no account agree to advance to the Belgian-German frontier. Churchill, however, stated a more probable dilemma: if the French on the BEF's left advanced, Gort would be placed in an awkward position. It should be possible, thought Churchill, to reach the Scheldt line. The Cabinet was reluctant to allow the BEF to leave prepared positions if there was a risk of being caught in the open, but concluded that the matter was a technical one and should be discussed by the Allied commanders. Gort and his Chief of Staff, Lieutenant General Sir Henry Pownall, shared Ironside's anxiety about any advance into Belgium, but for the moment the question was rather academic since the BEF had not yet taken its place in the line.[4]

By the end of September the Belgian Government had made it plain that it could not contemplate official staff conversations with either Britain or France for fear of compromising its neutrality. Indeed political and military reactions in Brussels were alike hostile to the Allied overtures, General Van Overstraeten, the King's miliary adviser, going so far as to describe the British proposals as '*enfantines*'. The Belgian view was that a German invasion was not inevitable and if one occurred it would be stoutly resisted. If official contacts with the Allies leaked out they would provide a perfect pretext for an immediate German attack. Moreover, the Allied forces available for the support of Belgium, particularly the BEF, were ludicrously weak in comparison with the enemy, so that Belgium would risk becoming a

---

[4] *Ironside Diaries* pp. 107-8, 112-13 and Appendix pp. 394-5. Cab 65/3 19(39)5, 18 September; 20(39)5, 19 September; 29(39)5, 27 September. Cab 66/1 WP (39) 33, 18 September. *Harvey Diaries* p. 319. Brian Bond (ed.) *Chief of Staff: the Diaries of Lieutenant General Sir Henry Pownall Vol I 1933-1940 op. cit.*, pp. 234-7.

battlefield to no good purpose. On 10 October the British Foreign Secretary informed the Cabinet that staff conversations were definitely not possible. Moreover, King Leopold now thought such conversations would be unwise and dishonourable: 'the Belgian Government appeared to be distressed that we should have placed them in an embarrassing position by asking them questions which they did not wish to answer'.

However, the Allied overtures did not meet with a complete rebuff because the Belgian General Staff, and to a lesser extent the King and General Van Overstraeten, saw the need to continue unofficial military contacts with the Allies in order to ensure that the latter would feel confident enough to advance into Belgium if invited. A solution was found in the convenient distinction between the political sphere of the Government and the purely military sphere of the King as Commander-in-Chief. Gamelin acknowledges in his memoirs that from the end of September 1939 he resumed unofficial contacts with the Belgians and reached provisional agreement on certain conditions that must obtain before he would order an advance.

Nevertheless, from an operational viewpoint Gamelin's dissatisfaction with these limited contacts was entirely justified. As a colloquium of French and Belgian historians noted, in the autumn of 1939 there still remained a profound gulf between Belgian and Allied conceptions of the coming battle. The Belgians conveyed the impression that they would defend the line of the Albert Canal and the Meuse without thought of withdrawal until French reinforcements arrived, whereas the latter were extremely dubious about taking such an enormous gamble. Gamelin, moreover, feared that when the Belgians were driven back from their frontiers they would make straight for the fortress system of Antwerp, as in 1914. In fact the three divisions concerned were ordered (on 25 September) in such an eventuality to retire southward so as to link up with the advancing French, but this important information was not passed to Gamelin.[5]

As for Britain, on the day following the Belgian rejection of official talks, the Cabinet was puzzled to learn that King Leopold had requested Admiral Sir Roger Keyes—a long-standing friend of the Belgian Royal Family—to visit Brussels. Chamberlain and Churchill speculated whether the King was acting behind the back of his ministers; at this time it would be more acccurate to say that he was acting in advance of Cabinet policy. The British Cabinet and the CIGS welcomed the idea of the sixty-seven-year-old admiral as a special emissary, but although Sir Roger Keyes paid several important visits to Brussels this intermittent and amateur liaison work was a poor

---

[5] General Van Overstraeten *Albert I-Leopold III: Vingt Ans de Politique Militaire Belge 1920-1940* (de Brouwer, *circa* 1946) pp. 371-7 (henceforth referred to as *Overstraeten*). General M. Gamelin *Servir* (Paris: Plon, 1946 3 Vols) I pp. 86-7, III pp. 82-5 (henceforth referred to as *Servir*). Cab 65/3 43(39)10, 10 October. *Les Relations Militaires op. cit.*, pp. 86, 97, 162-3.

substitute for full staff talks. It was also not without its dangers in contributing to friction and misunderstanding.[6]

Admiral Keyes paid his first secret visit to Brussels from 17 to 21 October and on his return reported to the CIGS. He had explained to King Leopold that there was some difficulty in getting definite news of the state of Belgian defences, and that the Belgians must co-operate if they wished to get British help. The Allies were not going to venture out of their defences to risk an encounter battle in the lowlands of Belgium. The military attaché must be allowed to see what was going on. King Leopold expressed astonishment at discovering the British knew so little about the Belgian defences. The Military Attaché then arrived and assured Ironside that the Belgians were working all out on the line from Wavre to Namur and were erecting a steel anti-tank obstacle at the rate of about 300 metres a day (this report subsequently proved over-optimistic). The King had impressed on Keyes that he wanted this exchange of information kept absolutely in military hands, and Ironside gave a personal undertaking to do so. The French, the King said, had never ceased to press them for a military alliance and he was terrified of being accused of violating his neutrality and being invaded by the Germans.[7]

The goodwill generated by Keyes' first mission secured a comparatively cordial reception for Colonel Blake, the British military attaché in Brussels, when he was granted an interview with General Van Overstraeten on 26 October. The latter reassured Colonel Blake that there was no question of the Belgians being driven from their frontier defences by a *coup de main*, nor would the BEF be exposed to an encounter battle. The Belgians intended to hold the line of the Albert Canal without thought of retreat, but should there be a catastrophe a strong position was being prepared on the line from Antwerp to Wavre.[8] One may doubt whether Ironside was much comforted by Blake's report of this interview in which Van Overstraeten asserted that Belgium would be a much harder nut for Germany to crack than Poland.

Anglo-French strategy was significantly affected by the first major crisis occasioned by the threat of a German attack in the West. Unlike Ironside, who doubted whether a full-scale attack on the Western Front would be launched until the following spring, Gamelin, though with frequent changes of mind, expected a main thrust through the Low Countries to develop between 22 October and 10 November. In this hunch he was correct, for despite a marked lack of enthusiasm among his generals, Hitler ordered the move forward to jumping off points to begin on 5 November for an offensive

---

[6] *Servir I* p. 86. Cab. 65/3 44(39)10, 11 October; 46(39)6, 13 October; 47(39)5, 14 October. Roger Keyes *Outrageous Fortune: the Tragedy of Leopold III of the Belgians 1901-1941.* (Secker & Warburg, 1984) pp. 121-3. C. Aspinall-Oglander *Roger Keyes* (Hogarth Press, 1951) pp. 343-4. *Ironside Diaries* pp. 115-16.
[7] *Ironside Diaries* pp. 132-3. For the Military Attaché's subsequent report that the Belgians were not after all fortifying the line Namur-Wavre see Cab 65/4 78(39)4, 10 November. *Overstraeten* pp. 388-9.
[8] *Overstraeten* pp. 392-5.

planned to begin on 12 November. In addition to the conspicuous troop movements on their frontiers and increased German air reconnaissance, the Belgian and Dutch Governments received warnings from Berlin of the impending attack. One consequence was that on 7 November the King of the Belgians and the Queen of the Netherlands issued a joint appeal to the belligerents to accept mediation. Another was that the Belgian Foreign Minister, Spaak, asked Gamelin what would be the French attitude if Germany attacked Holland but not Belgium: would the French wish the Belgians to invite them in or prefer them to stay neutral? The Belgians were also of course interested in what steps the Allies would take to support them against aggression; but it was the revival of this old problem of support for Holland that gave a new twist to Allied discussions on strategy.

Before turning to examine those discussions it should be noted that deteriorating weather conditions caused, on 7 November, the German attack to be postponed for three days, and it was subsequently revived and postponed no less than fourteen times. The monarchs' joint appeal had no practical outcome, and once the crisis appeared to have passed—by mid-November—the Belgians' short-lived enthusiasm for co-operation with the Allies declined. On 11 November the British Ambassador in Paris, Sir Ronald Campbell, reported that the Belgians were again blowing cold on staff talks and the French were not after all sending a general to Brussels. 'The French were evidently somewhat exasperated by this shilly-shallying and feared that when the threat materialized and the Belgians appealed, the French would not have time to render effective help'. It was mistakenly believed that the King was holding back his Cabinet from staff conversations.[9]

The most important consequence of this false alarm was that it once again focused Gamelin's attention on the possibility of military support for Holland, and led to the adoption of the more ambitious strategy which was, in fact, implemented on 10 May 1940. Early in November Gamelin conceived the project, in the event of Belgium inviting the Allies in 'en temps utile', of thrusting forward a French motorized force on his extreme left flank to occupy the Dutch territory on both shores of the Scheldt estuary, including the islands of Walcheren and South Beveland, and linking up with the Belgian garrison of Antwerp. On the right, or southern flank of this force, Gamelin intended at the least to advance to the line of the Scheldt. For the BEF this would involve a forward move of only about five miles on their right and thirteen on their left. Gamelin remained adamant that he would not move at all unless invited in and would not risk an encounter battle. If, however, time permitted, Gamelin did now contemplate a further advance beyond the

---

[9] *Ibid* pp. 405-6. *Butler* pp. 160-1. Roger Parkinson *Peace for our Time: Munich to Dunkirk—the inside story* (Hart-Davis, 1971) pp. 265-6 (henceforth referred to as *Parkinson*). Cab 65/4 79(39)9, 11 November. For a vivid account of the German generals' opposition to a Western offensive in November 1939 see Harold C. Deutsch *The Conspiracy against Hitler in the Twilight War* (Minneapolis, 1968).

Scheldt but stopping short of the Albert Canal. This intermediate line was that of the river Dyle (Namur-Wavre-Antwerp) which became known as 'Plan D' (Dyle) and remained an alternative to the more cautious 'Plan E' (Escaut or Scheldt).

'Plan D' had several advantages over remaining on the French frontier or advancing only to the Scheldt. It would reduce the total front defended by the Allies in the West by seventy or eighty kilometres, thus (in theory) freeing more troops for a central reserve (in practice it had the opposite result). It would save more Belgian territory—particularly the industrial regions—and would deepen the zone of anti-aircraft defences. It increased the chances of linking up with the twenty-odd divisions of the Belgian field army and perhaps also of absorbing some Dutch units when they retreated. In the long defence of this plan in his memoirs, Gamelin argued that these advantages far outweighed the disadvantages of leaving well-known defences to advance to dubious positions, with the concomitant danger of air attack during the forward move. He also argued that he had made ample provision of reserves to balance the motorized divisions employed on the dash into Holland on the left flank, but this was hardly borne out by the events of May 1940. Two other points in Gamelin's later self-justification merit special emphasis. He believed that Britain would feel her interests to be more deeply involved in the direct defence of Belgium than she did in France and would be more likely to commit her reserves. Also he saw the advanced line in Belgium as providing a better springboard for eventual mobile offensive operations than the Maginot Line.[10]

Gamelin's projected plans were discussed at a top-level military conference at Vinçennes on 9 November. Among those present were Gamelin, Georges, Gort, Pownall, Ironside and Newall (the Chief of Air Staff). In view of Ironside's previous hostility to any advance into Belgium it might have been anticipated that he would strongly object to 'Plan D'. He seems, however, to have accepted Gamelin's undertaking that he would not risk an encounter battle, and was perhaps also reassured by the information—subsequently refuted by the British military attaché in Brussels—that the Belgians were working hard to fortify the sector between Wavre and Namur.

Pownall thought the project to support Holland 'rather ambitious' but he added in his diary a comment which he overlooked when subsequently accounting for the Allied defeat: 'It is good of the French to worry about Walcheren, whose denial to the enemy is primarily a British interest'.[11] If Gort had any reservations he suppressed them in the interests of Allied unity. Gamelin had been accommodating as to the sector on the French frontier to

---

[10] *Servir I* pp. 89-108.
[11] Cab 65/4 77(39)1, 9 November and Cab 80/6 COS (39) 162 Annex V. *Pownall Diaries* pp. 252-4. Cf Pownall's reference in his Retrospect, written in June 1940, to 'Gamelin's major strategical blunder, made in cold blood months ahead. It was *the role of the Seventh Army in the North*' (diarist's emphasis). A choice example of wisdom after the event.

be garrisoned by the BEF, and in return Gort stressed that he was under French orders and would advance when told to without reference to the British Government. In sum, none of the British military experts spoke out against a project which was subsequently thought to have contributed largely to the débacle in May 1940.

On his return to England on 9 November, Ironside was summoned straight to a War Cabinet meeting where his advice was sought on whether the BEF could advance. The CIGS pointed out that the British Government had expressly placed Lord Gort under the orders of the French High Command, but with the right of appeal to the Cabinet. Since he had not exercised this right, it would be unwise for the Cabinet to interfere. The Cabinet accepted the soldier's viewpoint.

On the whole the War Cabinet was in favour of the French trying to aid the Dutch by seizing the Scheldt estuary and islands, though the operation was not thought to be vital since even if successful it would not guarantee the security of Antwerp.[12]

This unenthusiastic attitude to Gamelin's Holland project was underlined by the Joint Planning Committee of the CID, which commented on 10 November:

> We do not consider that the occupation of the islands of Walcheren and South Beveland could have any effect in reducing the scale of naval or air threat to this country, consequent upon the German occupation of Holland. Nor would it appear that the presence of French troops in these islands would be sufficient either to provide adequate cover to the left flank of the Belgian defence, or to afford us the use of Antwerp. Nor is it necessary to occupy the islands to deny the use of the waterway to the Germans.

The Committee felt that the best French plan would be to occupy Dutch territory on the south bank of the Scheldt and try to strengthen the Belgians' left. Britain could do little to assist the French in this venture and no British troops would be available. They pointed out that although the BEF was under French orders, they were confident that it would not be committed to an encounter battle. Their report was approved in a Chiefs of Staff Memorandum dated 18 November.[13] Thus, although the British planning experts were unimpressed by the Dutch aspect of 'Plan D', no direct criticism was relayed to Gamelin. Gort's acquiescence, backed by Ironside, does indeed seem to have 'quietened down' the Cabinet.

After receiving assurances from the Belgian military authorities regarding their state of mobilization and construction of defences on 13 November, Gamelin expounded his plan to the British and French commanders at Georges' headquarters on the following day. Briefly the French Ninth and First Armies would hold the line of the Meuse from Givet to Wavre; the

[12] Cab 80/6 COS (39) 162 Annex V. Cab 65/4 77(39)1, 9 November. *Ironside Diaries* p. 157.
[13] Cab 66/3 WP(39)123, 13 November enclosing COS (39)117 (J.P.). Report by the Joint-Planning Committee on a German invasion of Holland and the French project to occupy Walcheren and South Beveland. See also *ibid* WP(39)136.

British would hold the line of the Dyle from Wavre to Louvain; the Belgians would occupy the sector between Louvain and Antwerp-Ghent; while the French Seventh Army would advance on the extreme left to guard the southern shore of the Scheldt and, if possible, link up with the Dutch forces. General Pownall noted in his diary that the Dyle line was 'vastly better than the river Escaut on which to fight a battle, it's a better position and has a good wad of territory behind it'. Administratively there would be problems in moving the BEF eighty miles forward in a hurry—'But of course it can be done and if we can bring it off neatly would be an excellent move'.[14]

Gamelin's plan was endorsed by the British and French Governments at a meeting of the Supreme War Council on 17 November. Both Prime Ministers spoke in favour of 'Plan D': Chamberlain urged the importance of saving as much Belgian territory as possible from German occupation; while Daladier was reported as having said that he regarded the defence of Antwerp-Namur as being as important as the defence of France itself. It should be stressed that 'Plan E' (Escaut or Scheldt line) remained a possible option, but henceforth 'Plan D' was agreed to be preferable if circumstances permitted.

Meanwhile, despite the brief period of closer relations early in November, Belgian attitudes towards the Allies remained cool and ambivalent. Sir Roger Keyes, who paid a second visit to the Belgian Court from 12-17 November, reported in the following terms after an interview with Queen Elizabeth. She was not prepared to say that Belgium would declare war if Holland were to be invaded. Her son, King Leopold, was unpopular in Paris and the French had caused difficulties ever since the last war. She had unbounded confidence in General Van Overstraeten (who, she said, was pro-Ally in sympathy and was the outstanding figure in the Belgian Army). Van Overstraeten was said to be on good terms with the British military attaché, but not with the French. The Belgians had evidently told Keyes that they wished this secret liaison to be confined to the British, because Ironside pointed out that this was practically impossible seeing that the BEF was subordinated to the French command.[15]

The Belgians, and Van Overstraeten in particular, were now pressing the Allies to agree to the far more hazardous advance to the Albert Canal, where they expected to hold out for at least a week. Van Overstraeten, for example had asked the British military attaché what support the British could bring to the defence of the Albert Canal within forty-eight hours and what further support would be available within the first four days. Ironside, clearly irritated, told the War Cabinet that Overstraeten was constantly asking what assistance could be given in certain circumstances while at the same time refusing to furnish particulars regarding his plans, disposal of troops and the length of time he would occupy selected positions. In support of Ironside,

---

[14] *Butler* p. 162. *Pownall Diaries* p. 255.
[15] Cab 65/4 87(39)6, 18 November. Keyes *Outrageous Fortune, op. cit.*, pp. 123-5.

Colonel Blake had recently reported that no defences had yet been made on the line Namur-Wavre. A steel anti-tank obstacle on the line Hal-Ninove was being taken up and would probably be re-erected on the Namur-Wavre line. Pownall, informed of the Belgian request by Colonel Blake, noted that it would be folly on Gamelin's part to risk an encounter battle because of 'political pressure, a sentiment or for the *beaux yeux* of the Belgians'. 'They had a good chance to ask us in way back in September and didn't take it. Now they'll get what help *we* think it is useful to give'. Keyes revealed the depth of Belgian suspicion of the French when he reported to Churchill that the Belgians were apprehensive that if the French occupied Liège they would not give it up again.[16]

So the year ended with the Western Front apparently all quiet. Gamelin had evolved a daring plan which had been approved by Britain (and tacitly by the Belgians) without its possible drawbacks—particularly Allied ignorance of Dutch war plans—having been fully examined. Superficially relations with the Belgians—on the military level at least—appeared to be cordial, but deep resentments and misunderstandings festered on all sides. These would increase rather than diminish as the 'Phoney War' dragged on into the new year.

Although the minutes and memoranda of the British War Cabinet in the first three months of the war are crammed with critical references to Belgium's obstinacy and shortsightedness in refusing overt military co-operation for the collective defence of Western Europe against German aggression, it is easy to sympathize with the Belgians in their well-nigh hopeless position. Oliver Harvey stated the Belgian case succinctly in his diary entry for 13 November:

> Poor Leopold is in a desperate dilemma. If he commits himself to a military agreement, the Germans will say he has violated his neutrality and so justify German invasion. If he doesn't get agreement with us and France we cannot afford him proper help if he is attacked—a vicious circle. Moreover, it can be represented as an allied interest that Germany should not invade Belgium and therefore that Belgium should not provoke Germany. The answer is, I suppose, that Germany will invade Belgium if it suits, whatever Belgium does.

On the other hand one can appreciate why the Allies became increasingly irritated, with serious consequences when the time for joint operations arrived. First, in view of Germany's expansionist policy since at least the re-occupation of the Rhineland, suspicion of French territorial ambitions at Belgium's expense were surely excessive. Second, in the autumn of 1939, the Belgians were already tending to overplay a weak strategic hand given their stance of political neutrality: for example in demanding that the Allies advance as far east as the Albert Canal. Thirdly, and closely related to this, the Belgians were over-optimistic in believing they could hold up the Germans for a lengthy period at their frontier defences. In mid-November, for example,

[16] *Overstraeten* pp. 410-30 *passim*. Cab 65/4 87(39)4, 10 November and 81(39)5, 13 November. *Pownall Diaries* pp. 254-5.

Van Overstraeten told Keyes that if the Germans did come they would sustain a decisive defeat. Perhaps by the end of the year both parties were moving towards a compromise agreement: the Belgians ceasing to demand speedy French support on the Albert Canal, while Gamelin was genuinely bent on pushing as far forward as possible.[17] Lastly there is the question of King Leopold's personal and confidential initiatives conducted largely through his contacts with Keyes. The King of the Belgians retained more real constitutional authority than the British monarchy and his position was enhanced by his effective personal command of the armed forces. Unfortunately it was difficult for the British and French Governments to understand Leopold's complex relationship with his Cabinet and all too easy for them to interpret what was intended as a delicate personal and private enquiry as a reflection of firm Cabinet policy. It now seems clear that, so far from being pro-German—as some contemporaries alleged—the King was bolder than the majority of the Cabinet in attempting to secure military liaison with the Allies on a level which would not compromise his country's neutrality to the extent of provoking a German invasion. The most unrealistic and potentially dangerous aspect of the King's diplomatic activity—from an Anglo-French viewpoint—was that he, and some of his advisers were pro-British but not pro-French. It was hardly realistic, as the CIGS, Ironside, was obliged to point out, to ask the British to withhold information from secret Belgian sources from the French when the BEF had been placed under French command. Paradoxically, however, Gamelin appears to have enjoyed military contacts with the Belgian general staff the results of which he did not pass on to his ally. In sum, Anglo-French co-operation, even at the military level, was not as close as it might have been, and the partners' separate contacts with the Belgians provided a further source of suspicion and misunderstanding.

On the Allied side the French Government had taken an ultra-cautious line on the two main strategic options available to it in the opening weeks of the war when Germany was pre-occupied with Poland and comparatively vulnerable in the west. Generals Gamelin and Vuillemin had, with British endorsement, decided against either a determined land offensive against the Siegfried Line or a vigorous air offensive against the Ruhr. When the Germans failed to follow up the destruction of Poland by a speedy attack in the West, which Gamelin anticipated, the latter was increasingly impressed by the arguments in favour of advancing the Allies' defensive line as far as possible into Belgium—even including the south-west corner of Holland.

Some of the risks attending such a strategy—particularly as embodied in 'Plan D'—were foreseen. For example, Gamelin certainly foresaw the dangers of being attacked from the air whilst advancing, and the concomitant need to be certain of the routes of the advance and the prepared positions to be occupied. What does not appear to have been carefully studied was whether

---

[17] *Harvey Diaries* pp. 329-30. Cab 65/4 87(39)6, 18 November.

the foremost Allied divisions could be extricated from Belgium should the line be breached further to the south. Occasional references were made to a possible German thrust through the Ardennes, but if anyone realized that such a thrust could be carried out by tanks en masse or that the Meuse could be speedily crossed upstream from Namur their insight was not reflected in Gamelin's plan or directives. Curiously, in his meeting with Ironside on 6 October Gamelin came close to predicting the eventual direction of the main German thrust, but he seems subsequently to have ruled out this possibility. According to Colonel Macleod's notes on the meeting, Gamelin appreciated that one avenue of approach open to the enemy was to penetrate Luxembourg and advance through the Ardennes south of the Meuse. However, he believed (wrongly) that such a difficult operation would take a long time to mount, and he also had considerable faith in the strength of the Belgian defences.[18]

Lastly, although British military experts were unenthusiastic about that aspect of 'Plan D' which called for an advance to the Scheldt estuary and beyond by the French Seventh Army under General Giraud, they did not apparently realize that Gamelin had virtually deprived himself of his central reserve and all for a project that was uncharacteristically quixotic.[19]

As an ironic finale to the unexpectedly inactive conclusion of the year 1939 on the Western Front, the British Secretary of State for War, Leslie Hore-Belisha, was removed from office over 'the pill-box affair': a conflict of opinion with his generals which had its origin in his tactless criticism of the slow progress of the British sector's defences on the Franco-Belgian frontier after a visit he had paid in late November. Hore-Belisha's position had long been precarious and this rather sordid episode provided the opportunity for his removal from office.

Lord Gort and his Chief of Staff were furious to learn that Hore-Belisha had raised the matter in the Army Council and at the War Cabinet. They began to press for his dismissal on the grounds that he had lost the confidence of the Army. The Prime Minister at first resisted this pressure, but apparently changed his mind on hearing from Lord Halifax that the War Minister was also unpopular with certain sections of the Foreign Office. Early in January 1940 Hore-Belisha was astonished to be offered the Board of Trade, especially as he had recently been assured that the Prime Minister had complete confidence in him. Although puzzled by Chamberlain's inadequate explanation, he might perhaps have accepted, but he was deeply

---

[18] *Macleod Papers.* Colonel Roderick Macleod, Ironside's Military Assistant at this time and later senior editor of his diaries covering the years 1937-1940, has kindly made available to me all his Papers relating to Lord Ironside. Unfortunately I have not been permitted to see the original diaries. On the meeting between Gamelin and Ironside on 6 October, 1939 see also Ellis pp. 317-18.
[19] *Butler* p. 163. For Gamelin's self-justification see *Servir I* pp. 81-108. On 12 October Ironside concluded that the main German attack would come through Luxembourg and Belgium south of the Meuse. *Ironside Diaries* p. 125.

hurt to discover that Churchill had been informed of the proposed changes before himself. He therefore chose to resign and was succeeded by Oliver Stanley.

At the time it was widely appreciated that the 'pill-box' controversy was merely the pretext rather than the true cause for Hore-Belisha's departure, but even so the full irony of the episode was missed. By the time of his dismissal it should have been clear to all parties concerned that the BEF would be committed to action well in advance of this line and would probably never use it at all.[20]

But these domestic troubles apart, the end of the year seemed to promise at least a further three months of inactivity in which the Western Front could be rendered virtually impregnable against a repetition of *blitzkrieg*.

[20] On the fall of Hore-Belisha see I. Macleod *Neville Chamberlain* (Muller, 1961); *Pownall Diaries* p. 256ff; D. Dilks (ed) *The Diaries of Sir Alexander Cadogan (Cassell, 1971)*, pp. 238, 241-4. A. J. Trythall 'The Downfall of Leslie Hore-Belisha' in *Journal of Contemporary History* Vol. 16 (1981) pp. 391-411.

2

The Mechelen Incident
and its Aftermath
10 January-10 May 1940

On the morning of 10 January 1940 a German courier aircraft, travelling from Munster to Cologne, lost its way in dense fog and crash-landed near Mechelen-sur-Meuse in Belgian territory. The passenger, Major Hellmuth Reinberger, a first-grade staff officer of 7 Airborne Division, first attempted to burn his papers behind a hedge and then, when taken to the local military headquarters for questioning, thrust them into a stove, only to be thwarted again by the prompt reaction of his interrogator, Captain Rodrique. Several pages were scorched beyond recognition but enough of the charred fragments remained to reveal that these were highly secret German plans for an imminent offensive in the West—actually set for 17 January, though the date had not been inserted. Although the papers were concerned with air force operations, they indicated that the offensive would be launched on a broad front between the North Sea and the Moselle. The German Sixth Army would cross the Maastricht appendix and advance into central Belgium while parachutists seized the Meuse bridges south of Namur.[1]

The Belgian military authorities at first naturally suspected a 'plant' or *ruse de guerre* designed to make them reveal their plans and perhaps invite the Allies in, thus providing the perfect pretext for a German invasion. However this supposition soon had to be abandoned in the face of overwhelming evidence that the plans were genuine. First it would have been difficult to fake the crash and, again, the reactions of the two officers seemed entirely plausible. Major Erich Hoenmanns, a reserve officer, was making an illicit journey simply to clock up more flying hours, while his passenger, Reinberger, a zealous career officer, had no business to be carrying secret plans by air. Both men appeared to be cast into despair by their misfortune. Furthermore, the German air attaché to Belgium and the Low Countries, General Wenniger,

[1] J. Vanwelkenhuyzen 'L'alerte du 10 janvier 1940' in *Revue d'histoire de la 2é guerre mondiale*, Oct 1953 pp. 33-54. *Les Relations Militaires, op. cit.*, 102-14. For photographs of fragments of the captured plans see *Overstraeten* facing pp. 450, 452 and *Belgium: the official account of what happened 1939-1940* facing pp. 88-9.

showed great anxiety in demanding to see the captives at once. He was refused permission until the Belgians had installed hidden microphones in the room, and when admitted the following morning his first question was to enquire if Reinberger had destroyed the documents. The latter untruthfully assured him that he had.

The captured documents served to corroborate rumours and warnings of an impending German offensive coming from other sources, including King Leopold's sister Princess Marie-José, wife of the Italian Crown Prince, the Vatican and Sweden. Most circumstantial of all, on 13 January the Belgian military attaché in Berlin, Colonel Goethals, informed Brussels in a coded message that a 'sincere informer' had warned him that the Germans would attack the following day. We now know that his immediate informant was Colonel J. Sas, the Dutch military attaché in Berlin who had been tipped off, as in the November alert, by Colonel Hans Oster one of the anti-Nazi conspirators in the *Abwehr*.[2] The repercussions of this information will shortly be examined, but first it needs to be stressed that the contents of the captured documents served to reinforce the Belgian high command's own well-informed intelligence estimates concerning Germany's military dispositions.

Until November the Belgians had anticipated that the Germans would attempt to repeat the Schlieffen Plan of 1914, with the main blow falling to the north of Liège. Since then, however, there had been increasing evidence of troop concentrations further south between the Moselle and the Rhine from Coblenz to Bonn, and along the frontiers of Belgium and Luxembourg. The Belgian consul-general at Cologne, anticipating the actual plan which Manstein was elaborating with remarkable insight, repeatedly warned that the Germans were preparing an attack through the Ardennes with the ultimate objective of Calais. The Belgian ambassador in Berlin also correctly diagnosed that the Germans were preparing to launch a massive glider and parachute attack behind the lines. The Belgian high command deduced that the Germans would attempt a double envelopment comprising two deep thrusts, one on the axis from Maastricht to Brussels, and the other from St Vith to Chimay. In the classic style of the German general staff, this operation would seek to destroy the Belgian and British armies and as much of the French as possible in the forward zone of Belgium and north-eastern France. Success clearly depended on surprise and the speedy capture of the Meuse bridges between Namur and Givet.[3]

The partial exposure of the German plan and the expectation that it was about to be implemented again focused attention on Belgium's tight-rope act of attempting to maintain her neutrality between two hostile camps. If the Germans were indeed about to march then steps must be taken to ensure that the Allies would intervene immediately afterwards, but so long as there was

[2] William L. Shirer *The Collapse of the Third Republic* (Pan Books ed, 1972), pp. 649-51.
[3] 'L'alerte du 10 janvier 1940' *op. cit.*, pp. 46-7.

the remotest chance of postponement—and the weather had been very bad—neither the King nor his Government were willing to risk provoking an attack. They also wanted to keep the Germans guessing as to how much they had discovered. On the evening of 11 January, therefore, General Van Overstraeten conveyed to the French and British military attachés a general idea of the contents of the seized documents. He did not divulge how the documents had been captured nor did he hand over copies or photographs but merely a two page *resumé* which he had made himself. He stressed that the information was intended only for General Gamelin in his capacity as military leader of the two countries who had guaranteed Belgium's territorial integrity.

Gamelin's lukewarm reaction to this information at a council of war held at Vinçennes on the morning of 12 January is understandable. The Low Countries had already cried 'wolf' on several occasions and this seemed a most unlikely time of year for Hitler to risk an all-out offensive. Moreover, Gamelin's Chief of Military Intelligence, Colonel Rivet, reported that his office was ignorant of any preparations for an immediate attack. (British GHQ in France was equally sceptical.) Gamelin lamented the Belgians' failure to show his assistant attaché, Colonel Hautcoeur, the original documents or to explain how they had come by them. He nevertheless ordered an immediate alert for the bulk of the front-line units of the French army which were to advance to the Belgian frontier ready to move in at a moment's notice. The following day General Laurent, the French military attaché in Brussels, reported that the Belgian alarm was based on more information than the captured documents (ie the telegram from Berlin); and at 1.30 am on Sunday 14 January Gamelin was woken to be told that 'a German attack is almost certain today'. General Ironside, the British CIGS was similarly alerted in the early hours of 14 January.[4]

Meanwhile there had begun a bizarre essay in secret diplomacy which served largely to increase the mistrust and misunderstanding between the Allies and the Belgians. King Leopold had been concerned, at least since November 1939, that if Belgium was to be drawn into war—as he saw it—on others' behalf, she should receive formal assurances in advance analagous to those received in 1914. Essentially this involved the guarantee that Belgium and her colonial territories would be fully restored after the war. The Belgian Foreign Minister, Spaak, opposed the King's idea of a formal appeal for guarantees in December 1939 on the grounds that it would entangle Belgium in an alliance, and he repeated this view when the King again mooted the idea on 11 January. Furthermore, the Cabinet was not unanimously pro-Ally. Leopold therefore decided to use Admiral Sir Roger Keyes as a personal

---

[4] *Ibid* pp. 48-50. *Overstraeten* p. 449ff. *Pownall Diaries* entries dated 13 and 14 January 1940. *Ironside Diaries* p. 205. Shirer pp. 650-2.

emissary to the British Government: he did not intend his enquiry to be revealed to the French.[5]

Admiral Keyes arrived at the royal palace at Laeken, via Gort's headquarters, on the evening of 13 January. Van Overstraeten records that since Belgium was about to become a battlefield 'principally for the sake of England' it was time for the latter to make a gesture by giving the following guarantees:

1. To re-establish the independence of Belgium and her colonies.
2. Not to treat for peace independently of Belgium.
3. To promise assistance in re-establishing Belgium's economy.

According to Van Overstraeten, the Admiral said he would go to London immediately and would return the next day with the guarantees. He drove back to Gort's headquarters, arriving in the early hours of 14 January but bad weather prevented him from flying to London. He therefore telephoned Churchill, then First Lord of the Admiralty. After giving the three conditions Keyes added the crucial gloss that 'If these conditions were agreed to, (he) Sir Roger thought that the King of the Belgians would be able to persuade his Minister (sic) to invite French and British troops into Belgium at once'.[6] This was the assumption—that it was Leopold's intention and not merely Sir Roger's hope—which was to cause so much exasperation and ill will. Keyes may not have been sufficiently explicit, but it is also possible that Churchill misheard or misunderstood the vital part of the message.

It was impossible to get a full Cabinet together at short notice on a Sunday morning, but a quorum assembled with Lord Chatfield, as Minister for the Co-ordination of Defence, in the chair at 12.30 pm. Churchill reported that he had conveyed Leopold's terms by telephone to the Prime Minister 'who had strongly disliked the suggestion that the Belgians should, at this late hour, attach conditions to receiving help from us. In the Prime Minister's view this was not a time for giving guarantees other than those implicit in a military alliance'. Oliver Stanley, who had just succeeded Hore-Belisha at the War Office, and who had been briefed by Ironside, was more impressed than the Prime Minister by the advantages the Allies would gain if the Belgians allowed them in before the Germans attacked. That this was their genuine intention received support from the news that the Belgians were removing barriers on the French frontier. Ironside strongly agreed with his War Minister: no doubt the Allied entry would provoke a German attack but even a few hours' start should enable them to get to the Wavre-Namur line. It was agreed that the Foreign Office should inform Daladier of Leopold's questions and discover the French attitude, while the CIGS should ask Gamelin how

---

[5] *Overstraeten* pp. 436, 439, 451. Keyes *Outrageous Fortune* pp. 132-6.
[6] *Overstraeten* pp. 457-60. Keyes *Outrageous Fortune* pp. 137-45. *Pownall Diaries* entry dated 13 January. Cab 65/11 12(40) 1, 14 January, 12.30 pm.

soon the Allies could advance into Belgium. Gamelin, meanwhile, ignorant of Leopold's initiative, was impatiently urging Gort to join him in entering Belgium and was extremely angry at the British Cabinet's failure to reach a decision.

The Cabinet met again at 6.30 pm, this time with the Prime Minister in the chair. Ironside assured the Ministers that the Allied forward motorized troops could reach the Namur-Antwerp line in about six hours, and occupation of the line should be completed in forty-eight hours. In his view, twelve hours' start over the Germans should be enough to ensure that the Allies would hold the line. The Prime Minister remained doubtful: he felt sure the Belgian Government would only invite the Allies in when they were quite certain a German attack was about to take place. Later Ironside noted the differing reactions of Churchill and Chamberlain during the crisis: the former, fully aware of the military value of entering Belgium, was enthusiastic and full of energy; the latter negative and angry at Belgium making conditions. The Cabinet agreed to send a qualified acceptance of the terms but pointed out that the guarantees exceeded the formal British commitment to France— a full ally—and furthermore it was impossible to be certain of fulfilling conditions after the war.[7]

The British reply was received with a mixture of outrage and scorn at the Belgian royal palace, if Van Overstraeten's account is anywhere near the truth. Chamberlain had been right on the essential issue: under no circumstances had the King intended to invite the Allies in before the Germans actually attacked. Britain's other misdemeanour in Belgian eyes had been to communicate the terms immediately to the French, who had accepted them unreservedly. Van Overstraeten explained to Keyes that for the Allies to anticipate a German attack would be wrong both politically and militarily; politically because Germany must clearly be seen to be the aggressor, (apparently the plans captured at Mechelen were not enough) and militarily because a prior move on the Allies' part would enable the Germans to disown the captured documents and subsequently change their plan. According to Van Overstraeten, Keyes reported that all the British generals, notably Dill (commanding I Corps) shared this military appraisal, ie, that it would be a mistake for the Allies to advance and reveal their hand. If Keyes did say this he was going too far. As we have seen, the CIGS was strongly in favour of entering Belgium, while Pownall, Chief of Staff of the BEF was, on balance, also in favour and one can presume that Gort shared his view. Furthermore, the British generals' opinion was of little significance since they were badly informed both as to German intentions and as to how much the Belgians knew.[8]

---

[7] Cab 65/11 12(40) 1 and 13(40) 1. *Ironside Diaries* pp. 205-8.

[8] *Overstraeten* pp. 462-6. Van Overstraeten's habit of meticulously noting the time of his numerous interviews and not simply the date lends an air of authority to his book, yet occasionally he is clearly in error. In particular on p. 466 he has Sir Roger Keyes describing a

Of course neither the King nor Van Overstraeten had ever actually told Keyes that if Britain accepted the guarantees the Allied troops would be admitted before the Germans attacked but, as he explained later, it was a not unreasonable extrapolation on his part considering that the invasion was expected on the 14th. Furthermore it was not apparent why the overture should have been made at all unless the Belgians had changed their policy and were willing to invite the Allies in at once. If Leopold needed additional guarantees to persuade his Government to summon the Allies in even after a German attack, one might conclude that the Cabinet was deeply divided or even pro-German. The Belgians were certainly trying to have their cake and eat it if, as Van Overstraeten claimed, 'ninety per cent of the population is pro-Ally in sentiment and desires passionately to remain out of the conflict'. Chamberlain told the Cabinet that the Belgian reply made a deplorable impression on him, since it appeared that the Belgians had never intended to invite the Allies to cross their frontier before the Germans invaded. Thus British feelings were ruffled and prejudices strengthened, while the King's foray into secret diplomacy designed 'to render a solution less difficult' had had the reverse effect.[9]

Misunderstanding leading to recrimination was, if anything, worse between the Belgians and the French. Gamelin, as we have seen, was more eager than Gort to take the bit between his teeth and enter Belgium, all the more so because he believed the Germans were not ready for an immediate attack and would therefore be slow to react. Above all, his greatest worry, that his vulnerable columns would be blasted to pieces by the Luftwaffe on the Belgian roads, was diminished by the snow and fog which would handicap if not prevent flying. He therefore assembled the French forward units along the Belgian frontier on 14 January, ignoring the second thoughts of General Georges, who advised against entry, and fully expected to be invited in the following day. At 8.30 am on 15 January the French Government (in response to Gamelin's impatient demand for a decision) addressed a brusque note to the Belgians imploring them to face up to their responsibilities. Every hour was precious; troops, horses and vehicles were waiting in the open under appalling conditions and could not be kept at the ready indefinitely. In any case the Germans would soon discover the Allied state of alert and then it would be too late. The note concluded with the scarcely veiled threat that if the Belgians missed this opportunity they must not expect the Allies to be so ready to come to their aid in future crises. Predictably, the Belgians were

a British Cabinet meeting at which he (Sir Roger) was present and spoke. Other sources show that Sir Roger did not return to England during the crisis and this is confirmed by his son, the present Lord Keyes. Nor is there any reference to Keyes being present in the War Cabinet minutes, which include visitors as well as *ex officio* members.

[9] Cab 65/11 15(40)7, 16 January. Cab 66/6 WP(40) 98, 12 March. *Overstraeten* pp. 465-6. *Cadogan Diaries* pp. 246, 249.

not swayed by this quasi-ultimatum. Gamelin did not learn of the Belgians' terse rejection of the French request until 8.30 pm on 15 January. It was a moment of bitter disappointment as he recalls in his memoirs: 'Je ne cache pas au président (Daladier) qu'à mon sens la Belgique a, une fois de plus, failli au destin. Pourvu que son attitude ne pèse pas sur la nôtre'!

Gamelin, like the British Government, found it difficult to perceive any logic in King Leopold's diplomacy. He concluded that the explanation must be that when Keyes had first been contacted and asked to sound out Britain about guarantees, the Belgians had really expected an attack on the 14th but that by the following day they were becoming reassured. This speculation probably hit the nail on the head, for at 2.30 pm on 15 January Van Overstraeten had been informed by the Belgian attaché in Berlin that adverse weather conditions had caused the attack to be postponed. Loss of surprise, which Hitler considered essential, also probably influenced the decision.[10]

Gamelin's disappointment and chagrin were the greater because there had been practical evidence of Belgian willingness to co-operate on the frontier. Taking an extraordinarily bold personal initiative towards midnight on 13-14 January, the Belgian Chief of Staff, General Van den Bergen, had ordered the frontier barriers to be removed. In some districts his orders were obeyed and a French cavalry column actually entered Belgium. When Van Overstraeten heard of this, at 11.30 am on 15 January, he promptly countermanded the order and, with the strong approval of the King, issued another stating that any foreign detachments entering Belgium were to be resisted. It is interesting to note that this order, which could easily have led to fighting on Belgium's west front, was issued several hours before Van Overstraeten heard that the German offensive had been postponed. Van Overstraeten's diary entries convey the sense of relish—almost of glee—with which, on the King's instructions, he dismissed the unfortunate Van den Bergen from his post for taking a pro-Allied initiative. Moreover, when Gamelin proposed to send the head of a French military mission (General Champon) to Brussels, thus making the alliance public, Van Overstraeten curtly informed Colonel Hautcoeur (on the evening of 15 January) that 'the presence of this delegate at Brussels was neither desired nor desirable' ('ni souhaitée, ni souhaitable').

The French proceeded, with some reason, to blame the British for the misunderstanding while, according to Van Overstraeten, Keyes said he deplored the revised British note which he delivered on 17 January, adding 'Je voudrais la détruire, car elle constitue, comme la précédente, une faute énorme

---

[10] *Servir III* pp. 155-61. *Overstraeten* p. 465ff. The French note included the somewhat hectoring sentence: 'It would be a mistake to count on a repetition of the present stand-to at every alert; if the Belgian government declined the proposal (that French troops be admitted immediately, before an effective German attack), French troops would not quit their permanent positions until after the German army had actually entered Belgium'.

du Gouvernement Britannique'. At home, Sir Alexander Cadogan speculated that 'probably, old Keyes had got it all wrong' and the editor notes tersely 'He had'. As a conclusion to the unhappy diplomatic exchanges, Van Overstraeten informed Colonel Hautcoeur that 'less than ever' would the Belgian Government be ready to change its policy of neutrality. Spaak explained Belgium's military precautionary measures to the German ambassador and assured him that the Government would never commit the folly of calling the Allies into the country. The ambassador was mollified and concluded his dispatch:

> I should like to add that a representative of the Court, who is very close to the King, who is himself of German extraction and whose pro-German sentiment is known, told me yesterday that the King would never permit the Belgian government to depart from the clear line of a neutral policy...[11]

Thus the Mechelen affair, although it expired in anticlimax, exerted a harmful influence on Anglo-French-Belgian relations. Its significance as marking a critical point in the strategic planning of the belligerents is probably even more important in accounting for the outcome of the campaign in May and June.

As already mentioned, the German operational plan existing in January 1940 bore a superficial resemblance to the Schlieffen Plan of 1914. The aim of this operation as defined by the Army General Staff (OKH) on 19 October was: 'To defeat the largest possible elements of the French and Allied Armies and simultaneously to gain as much territory as possible in Holland, Belgium and Northern France as a basis for successful air and sea operations against Britain and as a broad protective zone for the Ruhr'. The decisive thrust was assigned to Army Group B, which would attack Belgium on both sides of Liège and simultaneously eliminate Holland. The covering role on its southern flank was given to Army Group A, whose twenty-two divisions contained no mechanized troops. General Erich von Manstein, Chief of Staff to Army Group A, who was critical of the plan from its inception, summed up its intentions as follows: 'The Anglo-French elements we expected to meet in Belgium were to be floored by a (powerful) straight right while our (weaker) left fist covered up. The territorial objective was the Channel coastline. What would follow this first punch we were not told'. Von Manstein was thoroughly dissatisfied with a plan whose object, contrary to Schlieffen's was merely partial victory and limited territorial gains. In any case the situation differed in two crucial respects from 1914: strategic surprise was virtually unattainable; and the French were unlikely to repeat the folly of a premature offensive in Lorraine. Surprisingly, the German generals had a high respect for Gamelin, but even allowing for their error of judgement, von Manstein was right in stressing that the OKH plan would lay the German northern wing open to a

---

[11] *Ibid*, pp. 464-88 *passim*. Shirer pp. 655-6. *Cadogan Diaries* p. 246.

large-scale counter offensive against its southern flank. Worse still, it was likely to result in a stalemate. Von Manstein gradually evolved an alternative plan designed to secure a decisive victory on land. Essentially he proposed to transfer the main role and the bulk of the armoured units (seven out of ten Panzer divisions) to Army Group A and to stake everything on a surprise attack through the Ardennes. Although by the end of November, 14 Motorized Corps had been moved up behind Army Group A's assembly area, Army Group B retained the major role, at least for the opening stages. (Hitler was never enamoured of the OKH plan and reserved the option of transferring the main effort to Army Group A.) Von Rundstedt, commanding Army Group A, made several attempts to persuade OKH of the superior merit of von Manstein's idea, but to no avail. Nor, it seems probable, did OKH pass on von Manstein's tiresome memoranda to Hitler.

Thus, as von Manstein notes, there was a certain irony in the fact that up to the Mechelen affair both the Allied and the German High Commands were opting for unadventurous strategies which, if implemented, would have led to a head-on clash in central Belgium. For the Germans an alternative lay in a risky drive through the Ardennes, the avenue of least expectation, whereas for Gamelin the alternative was to refrain from intervening in Belgium and to keep his mobile forces concentrated for a flank attack when the enemy became over-stretched.

Did the capture of their plan of operations at Mechelen cause a drastic revision of German strategy? Von Manstein asserts that it had no direct effect but may have helped indirectly by making Hitler and OKH more receptive to Army Group A's proposals later on. But von Manstein was an interested party and it seems likely that the episode did immediately affect Hitler's attitude. A Commander-in-Chief's conference at Bad Godesberg on 25 January made only minor changes in Army Group B's instructions and still refused to release the bulk of the armour to von Rundstedt. The loss of the operation order had apparently had no effect on the thinking of OKH. William Shirer stresses, however, that the German High Command was seriously disturbed by the loss of the plan and that in particular Hitler began to think of turning the misfortune to advantage by shifting the main thrust further south (towards Sedan) while encouraging the enemy to believe that Holland and Belgium remained the principal objectives.

Meanwhile Army Group A continued to press the weakness of the existing plan on OKH. Von Manstein recalls that after a sand-table exercise in Coblenz on 7 February, General Halder seemed impressed by the argument that if the French pushed strong mechanized units into southern Belgium the armour allotted to Army Group A (19 Panzer Corps) would be too weak either to overcome the enemy or force a crossing of the Meuse.

At this time (9 February) von Manstein left the Western Front to take up a home command—a dubious compliment from OKH—but his colleagues on the staff of Army Group A continued their efforts to draw Hitler's attention to what may fairly be called 'the Manstein plan'. On 17 February von Manstein was summoned to Berlin to report to Hitler in person and noted 'I found him surprisingly quick to grasp the points which our Army Group had been advocating for many months past and he entirely agreed with what I had to say'. Not only had Hitler discovered an able professional exponent of his own intuitive ideas, but belatedly OKH was also coming round to a similar solution. Consequently, on 20 February, a new (and final) Operation Order was issued embodying von Manstein's essential ideas. The main weight of the operation was transferred to the southern wing, but Army Group B (with three armies) remained strong enough to overrun Holland and northern Belgium. Army Group A's mission was to surprise the enemy by thrusting through the Ardennes and across the Meuse to the lower Somme. While guarding against a counterblow on the German southern flank it would also prevent the armies in Belgium from retreating across the Somme. Thus, prodded by Hitler, the German High Command profited from the Mechelen incident and its aftermath and by mid-February had evolved the daring plan which was to be brilliantly executed in May.[12]

When one turns to the French side the story is quite different. Not only the Mechelen affair, but a number of other considerations would seem to have made it imperative for Gamelin to adopt a more flexible strategy, yet to the last he stubbornly clung to the directive issued in mid-November for an advance to alternative positions in Belgium coupled with a powerful left-wing thrust into Holland. The best that can be said for Gamelin—and it is not an impressive defence—is that he allowed semi-political considerations to outweigh practical operational factors. However, the unavoidable charge remains that he failed to make allowance for the enemy attempting the unexpected or even changing his plan.

The first count against Gamelin is that he persisted in his plans despite the repeated criticism of his subordinates who would have to implement them, in particular Generals Georges, Billotte and Giraud. On 14 November, before Gamelin's project had been finally approved by the Supreme War Council, Georges voiced his reservations about pushing forward into Belgium: 'We cannot push on from the Scheldt to the Antwerp-Namur position (he argued) unless the Command feels ... it can reach the position *before* the enemy and organize it before the enemy is able to attack it in force'. On 5 December Georges forwarded to Gamelin the critical observations of Billotte and Giraud. They pointed out that as there was no joint-planning between the Belgians and the Dutch there would be no common defence north of Antwerp and, worse still, there was a strong probability that the Germans would reach Breda before the French. Georges himself hit on the key problem in

[12] Erich von Manstein *Lost Victories* (Methuen, 1958), pp. 97-100, 118-23. Shirer pp. 657-9, 675. Ellis pp. 335-44. J. J. Mearsheimer *Conventional Deterrence* (Ithaca N.Y.: Cornell University Press, 1984), pp. 99-133.

suggesting, that, contrary to current assumptions, the Low Countries might not turn out to be the decisive theatre: 'There can be no doubt that our defensive manoeuvre in Belgium and Holland will have to be conducted with the thought that we must not be drawn into engaging in this theatre, in face of a German move which might be merely a diversion, the major part of our available forces. If, for example, the main enemy attack came in our centre, on our front between the Meuse and the Moselle, we could be deprived of the necessary means to repel it'. In the spring of 1940 the French High Command learnt that the Dutch intended to abandon their eastern frontiers in the event of attack and attempt to hold Fortress Holland around Amsterdam, Rotterdam and The Hague. This rendered the French Seventh Army's mission pointless, but renewed objections to this and to other aspects of Gamelin's plan were ignored and it was made final on 15 April.[13]

Gamelin's position would be somewhat less vulnerable had it been merely a question of his intuition against that of his critics. Unfortunately for his reputation as a strategist, a wide variety of intelligence sources increasingly indicated (between November 1939 and the end of April 1940) the probability that the main German attack would be launched south of the Belgian Meuse in the general direction of Dinant-Sedan.

Even before the Mechelen affair Allied intelligence had noticed a pronounced southward movement of German units on the Western Front. In November 1939 between fifteen and twenty divisions were located opposite the Limbourg area in the Netherlands and twenty to twenty-five on the borders of Belgium and Luxembourg. Two months later the figures were respectively twenty to twenty-five against fifty-seven.

The distinguished Swiss military historian, Professor Eddy Bauer, has argued that a more critical examination of the charred fragments captured at Mechelen should have alerted French headquarters that the Germans were not contemplating a repetition of the Schlieffen Plan in which their main weight would be placed on the right wing driving through central Belgium. In particular the intended use of one of their two precious airborne units to capture and hold bridges upstream from Namur in the Dinant area might have suggested—if collated with other information as to the location of German armoured divisions—that a major thrust was to be made through the Ardennes. This seems unfair to the Deuxième Bureau at Vinçennes and La Ferté on two counts. First, contrary to Bauer's belief, the Belgians did not hand over photographs of the charred documents to the French but only a précis, which would have been far harder to interpret with precision. Secondly, as we have seen from von Manstein's account of his difficulties

---

[13] A. Goutard *1940: La Guerre des occasions perdues* (Paris: Hatchette, 1956), pp. 146-7. P. Lyet *La Bataille de France Mai-Juin 1940* (Paris: Payot, 1947), pp. 19, 22-6. Shirer pp. 663-8. In view of the importance he attached to the mission of French 7th Army, it is strange that Gamelin appears to have made little effort to persuade the Dutch to conform to his plan. See *Les Relations Militaires*, pp. 130-5, 171-2.

with OKH, the Ardennes thrust remained only a possibility until after the Mechelen incident.

Nevertheless the accumulated weight of information ignored by Gamelin remains formidable. In March 1940 Swiss military intelligence detected with a high degree of certainty six or seven Panzer divisions between the Moselle and the line Bonn-Euskirchen, compared with only three placed to operate north of Liège. This reading of the situation was borne out by the location of motorized units. Also, as Bauer points out, it was impossible to reconcile with a repetition of the Schlieffen Plan the eight bridges which the Germans had thrown across the middle Rhine between Bingen and Bonn; or the pontoons which German engineers were constructing over the rivers on the Luxembourg border and which caused a panic in the Grand Duchy. Indeed, on 1 April the famous French author-aviator, Antoine de Saint-Exupéry carried out a photographic reconnaissance of the Rhine bridges in a Bloch 141. Shortly before this, on 22 March, Colonel Paillole, chief of the German section of the Deuxième Bureau, reported that German intelligence officers had suddenly begun to study the routes from Sedan to Abbeville, seeking such information as the width of bridges, the nature of water obstacles and the condition of the roads. He deduced correctly that an attack across Belgium in the direction of the Channel and the North Sea was imminent. Finally, as late as 30 April, the French military attaché in Berne placed at Sedan the centre of gravity of a German offensive to be launched between 8 and 10 May. These repeated warnings seem to have had no effect on Gamelin.

Lastly, in justice to the Belgian High Command, it must be said that their reading of German intentions from the end of January was in the main sound, and that they did attempt to alert the French. On 8 March King Leopold pointed out to his principal ministers that Gamelin's plan to throw his left wing forward into Holland was a difficult manoeuvre from which success was virtually impossible. In attempting it he risked ruining the Allied left wing among the Zeeland estuaries, while a German riposte through the Ardennes towards Dinant-St Quentin would cut off the northern group of armies from Paris and roll them up in the Pas-de-Calais. General Van Overstraeten was authorized to reveal to Gamelin (via the Belgian military attaché) that documentary evidence in their hands led to the certain conclusion that the principal axis of the enemy's manoeuvre would lie perpendicularly on the front Longwy-Givet. Gamelin's headquarters at Vinçennes received this warning coolly and refused the Belgian attaché permission to visit the threatened area. Again, on 14 April, Van Overstraeten noted that the Germans planned to entice (aspirer) the Allies into Belgium and destroy them by an enveloping riposte from Luxembourg.[14]

[14] Eddy Bauer *La Guerre Des Blindés* (Lusanne: Payot, 1962, 2 vols), I pp. 86-91. *Overstraeten* pp. 520, 522, 555. On p. 484 Overstraeten records an interview with Colonel Blake on 25 January from which it is clear that the Belgians had so far been unwilling to hand over copies of the captured documents. Shirer pp. 688-70. Note that the author takes some liberties with his sources here; for example, Overstraeten does *not* say that he repeated the warning to the French on 14 April.

It is of course only too easy after a military disaster (and Pearl Habour provides an obvious analogy) to select those scattered items of intelligence which, if correctly pieced together in good time, would have enabled the defender to parry the blow. Conceivably the information flowing into Gamelin's headquarters could have been interpreted to fit a preconceived idea that the major blow would be delivered against Holland and Belgium. Nevertheless the indictment against Gamelin is damning: not merely was he mistaken about German intentions but he appears to have been unwilling even to consider the possibility of an armoured thrust through the Ardennes. As a result his weakest armies, Ninth and Second, were left to their fate on the Meuse and with no organized reserve behind them. One can only echo Professor Bauer, who quotes the adage 'Whom Jupiter wishes to destroy he first makes mad'.

While the British Government was still puzzling over what it had done to infuriate the Belgians over the Mechelen incident and King Leopold's overture, it was confronted with a crisis over the command of the Allied land forces in France. Although it was common knowledge that personal relations between Gamelin and Georges were strained, Lord Gort had assumed that their rivalry did not affect the BEF. Gamelin had delegated command of the BEF to Georges at the outbreak of war and this had been confirmed in a note from the military attaché in Paris on 3 September, 1939. Now, in February 1940, only a month after Georges had been confirmed as C-in-C of Allied forces on the north-eastern front, Gamelin asserted his right to direct command of the BEF, explaining that the latter was only subordinated to Georges for routine matters![15] Quite apart from the fact that the British generals principally concerned, Gort, Pownall and Ironside, much preferred dealing with Georges, there was an obvious danger of conflicting orders and muddle. After many tedious meetings over what Pownall over-complacently described as 'largely a storm in a teacup', new instructions were issued to Gort on 28 March. These confirmed that the BEF was under Gamelin, who might, if he wished, delegate command directly to Georges. In any case Gort would be permitted direct access to Gamelin. This arrangement was clearly a compromise to suit Gamelin but it rendered Georges's position difficult and augured poorly for the Allied command system when subjected to the stress of battle. When Gort and Pownall saw Georges early in March they heard that Gamelin had kept him completely in the dark about this issue. For the first time, Pownall recorded, 'I heard Georges speak with bitterness in his voice.

[15] Cab 66/5 WP(40)67 (enclosing Paper No. COS (40)239) 23 February 1940. *Ibid* 74 26 February, 99, 18 March; 113 28 March. Shirer pp. 602, 654n. *Pownall Diaries* pp. 277, 285-8. Pownall described the reorganization of French GQG as follows: 'A good part of 1st and 2nd Bureaux go to Gamelin though, absurdly enough, they don't go to Vincennes but near Meaux, where, out of touch with both Georges and Gamelin they function under (General) Doumenc. 3rd Bureau stays with Georges, 4th Bureau also stays with Georges but is under Gamelin and the head of it will be Gamelin! It's a really clownish arrangement'.

He and Roton (his Chief of Staff) were very quiet and depressed. I fear that there are other frictions of which we have heard nothing and that feeling is running very high...'[16]

This was indeed the case, for the antagonism between Gamelin and Georges was in part the reflection of the intense political rivalry between Daladier and Reynaud. Daladier championed Gamelin and was, according to the latter, 'always extremely cool towards Georges', who in turn was aware that the Premier detested him. When Reynaud became Premier in late March 1940 he soon determined to dismiss Gamelin ('this nerveless philosopher' as he derisively described him to Paul Baudouin on 12 April), but the general was obstinately defended by Daladier, who remained in the War Cabinet in the all-important post of Minister of National Defence. Paul Baudouin vividly describes the tragic and frightful War Cabinet meeting in which Reynaud strove in vain to secure Gamelin's dismissal: 'He stated his case in an icy silence under the frown of M. Daladier who sat there with his jaw set, and continually shrugging his shoulders. When the Prime Minister stopped, for a minute that seemed an hour, nobody spoke. Then in a deep and harsh voice, M. Daladier ranged himself with General Gamelin, and said it was the last time that he would attend a meeting of this nature'. Thwarted on this occasion, Reynaud redoubled his efforts to remove a C-in-C in whom he had no confidence whatever (by this time Georges too had made a poor impression and the likely replacement was the seventy-three-year-old Weygand). Finally, Reynaud determined to force the issue even at the cost of the resignation of his Cabinet. Since Daladier refused to yield, this crisis occurred on 9 May but was kept secret that day pending the formation of a new Cabinet. The German attack in the early hours of 10 May afforded a temporary respite for Reynaud—and Gamelin—but personal relationships in the French Government and High Command could hardly have been worse for the waging of a life-and-death struggle.[17]

In the knowledge of the outcome of the German onslaught on the Low Countries and France in May and June 1940 it now seems almost incredible that in the period from January to April inclusive the Allies were more concerned, one might fairly say obsessed, with extending the war to Scandinavia. 'It is extraordinary', Sir John Slessor wrote, 'to look back upon our blindness to the realities of a situation that was constantly obtruding itself upon our attention'.[18] So many arguments were entangled in the Scandinavian strategy

---

[16] *Pownall Diaries* p. 288.

[17] Paul Baudouin *The Private Diaries (March 1940-January 1941)* (Eyre and Spottiswoode, 1948), pp. 1-26. The British Government underwent a crisis at precisely the same time, not entirely by coincidence since both had been discredited by the fiasco in Norway. However, the British crisis did not immediately involve the High Command (though the CIGS was replaced shortly afterwards) and, unlike France, Britain discovered a magnificent war leader with strong Party and Parliamentary backing.

[18] Sir John Slessor *The Central Blue* p. 268ff. Butler pp. 107-8. R. A. C. Parker 'Britain, France and Scandinavia, 1939-40' in *History* Vol. 61 No. 203, October 1976 pp. 369-87.

that it is difficult to summarize them concisely. For the British, the principal justification was that if the German supply of iron ore from Sweden could be entirely cut off for one year the effect would be 'decisive', though whether this would have been the case is hard to say. A secondary argument, particularly espoused by the CIGS, Ironside, was that it would be to the Allies' advantage to divert German divisions to Scandinavia. The CIGS was quite certain that the Germans had lost the opportunity to attack on the Western Front. Moreover, he believed that if the Allies could get Germany embroiled in Scandinavia she would also forfeit the capacity to attack in the Balkans.[19] This depended on the false assumption that Germany was incapable of launching two widely separated operations simultaneously. The French may have subscribed to these arguments, but it is hard to avoid the feeling that they were anxious to end the inactive '*sitzkrieg*' in the West while ensuring that the action took place as far away from France as possible. In retrospect, in addition to the almost complacent underestimation of Germany's military potential to repeat the *blitzkrieg* on a larger scale, the most hair-raising aspect of the whole episode was the willingness of the Allies to add Russia to their enemies by supporting Finland. Nor does the morality of the Scandinavian policy bear too close a scrutiny. Fortunately the unwillingness of Sweden and Norway to co-operate, followed by Finland's collapse in March, saved the Allies from this strategic nightmare. But early in April the Allies carried the war into Norway (in the event a few hours after the German attack) with results which, at least in the short term, were disastrous.

On a wider view, the Scandinavian episode also marked an astonishing departure from the basic assumptions prevalent in the opening months of the war; namely that Germany was vastly more powerful than the Allies in the short run and would probably attempt to gain decisive results in the West. Allied strategy must therefore be defensive and avoid provoking Germany—for example by bombing the Ruhr—until her strength had been built up. One can only speculate that as well as the impatience for action (somewhere, anywhere), the frequent false cries of 'wolf' led some people to the comforting belief that Hitler had abandoned the idea of a Western offensive. This belief, as we have seen, was untenable for anyone *au fait* with the enemy's troop movements, and in any case should have been dispelled by the Mechelen incident.

One could hardly expect British GHQ in France to share this optimistic view that Hitler had 'missed the bus'. As early as 9 February Gort's Chief of Staff, Henry Pownall, justly described in his diary the scheme to aid Finland as 'harebrained'—'the child of those master strategists Winston and Ironside'. 'Of all the harebrained projects I have heard this is the most foolish—its inception smacks all too alarmingly of Gallipoli'. Its immediate

---

[19] *Macleod Papers* Ironside's diary entries on the planning of operations in Scandinavia make it easy to understand Pownall's sarcastic references to the 'Crazy Gang' of British strategists.

effect on the BEF was to delay the arrival of 42 and 44 Divisions of III Corps, while 5 Division was earmarked for withdrawal from France.

> To us here the business is deplorable. For five months we have been struggling to make fit for action in the spring a force that last September was dangerously under-equipped and untrained... As spring approached there were signs we were getting some reasonable way to our goal. By the end of this month we would have ten divisions, not nearly fully equipped, God knows, far from fully trained either, but still a force which in defence could make a good showing. If this business goes through (and the saving grace is that I don't believe it can) we shall be cut by three divisions, thirty per cent. It is a most disheartening business, but here at GHQ we mustn't show it for it would spread down and affect the morale of the force.

According to Pownall, neither Gort nor Georges had been consulted in advance as to whether they could carry out their responsibilities with a diminished force, yet as he foresaw 'Only on the Western Front can the war be lost on land, and there it can be lost in a few weeks if things went badly'. On 7 March Pownall expressed his disquiet over the Finnish project more graphically.

> Meanwhile the steady drain on our resources continues. Ammunition is not being despatched, transportation personnel is removed, the 5th Division has to be made up in a number of ways from resources out here, supply clerks and RAMC personnel ordered home. A continuous succession of items. The tide is setting *away* from us, which is very very depressing to us after all these months when we have been struggling to build up and train an efficient force out here, when we were within sight of that goal but had *by no means* reached it.

Between 17 March and 4 April, GHQ could again breathe freely with the Finnish venture definitely off, but on the latter date they were informed that the Norwegian operation had been resurrected. Not only would this entail delay in the arrival of troops, but also in the build up of stocks of gun ammunition, which was already badly behind schedule. Through the remainder of the month there was a steady trickle of men and equipment out of France to Britain for the Norwegian campaign. Pownall's bitter reflections (on 22 April) are understandable:

> We are still losing driblets away, not very much they may seem individually but collectively the sum mounts and mounts. No Bofors ammunition this month; no Kerrison predictors, (sighting apparatus which improved the efficiency of anti-aircraft guns) instead of the sixteen we had hoped for; two heavy AA Regiments earmarked to come if operations were to start will now *not* come; another regiment that was promised us for May is not coming; (15th) Brigade of 5th Division has gone (ordered home for dispatch to Norway) embarked thirty-six hours after the orders were received; transportation personnel in fives and tens: it all mounts up. HMG who up to a year ago would not accept that the Army would be called to fight in Europe at all are now running two European campaigns. It's the soldier who suffers and pays with his life for the purblindness of the politician and their refusal to look facts in the face or accept the advice of their proper advisers...[20]

[20] *Pownall Diaries* pp. 281-3, 288-91, 302. Ellis p. 33. The 15th Brigade of 5th Division was ordered home from France prior to embarkation for Norway on 15 April.

After a lull following the Mechelen incident, the agonizing problem of a preventative advance into Belgium was revived towards the end of March and reached a climax on 9-11 April when yet another German invasion scare flourished. Unrealistic as it seems now, there was a widespread belief that Germany might employ 'salami tactics' by invading the Netherlands but not Belgium. On 18 March the Belgian Foreign Minister, Spaak, enquired what the Allies would do in this eventuality. The British response, communicated to The Hague as well as to Brussels, was that if the Netherlands was attacked and Belgium supported her, the Allies would certainly go to Belgium's assistance. If, however, Belgium did not support her neighbour and the latter appealed for aid, the Allies would send air support and would also send troops into Belgium both to help the Netherlands and to protect themselves.[21]

Subsequently the British War Cabinet decided that in the event of a German attack on the Netherlands or Belgium British troops should advance into the latter whether invited or not, but that this intention should not be revealed to the Belgian Government, which was known to be agitated on the subject. This ruthless approach reckoned without its chief executant, Gamelin, who was reluctant to enter Belgium unless invited because, as he rightly pointed out, the Allies would have to advance about 100 miles into Belgium before aid to Holland could be effective and this would be impractical with a hostile population on their line of communications. Shades of the projected advance across Scandinavia to aid Finland! At a meeting between the Chiefs of Staff and the French High Command at Richmond Terrace on 27 March the British accepted Gamelin's viewpoint: he would not enter Belgium unless invited but could then do so without consulting the Allied governments.[22]

This agreement was short-lived. The alert on 9-11 April seems to have been the result of mixed motives: a genuine belief that the Germans were about to attack Holland and/or Belgium, or a desire to take advantage of Germany while she was preoccupied in Norway. At a War Committee meeting in Paris on 9 April, Admiral Darlan suggested that the Allied forces should move into Belgium if its government agreed. Generals Gamelin and Georges agreed with Darlan. The British Chiefs of Staff were still in favour of preventive action, for on 11 April they recommended to the French Government that the military authorities be authorized to take the following steps on the night before the German attack was due to commence:

1. The Allied Army was to advance into Belgium.
2. The Air Forces were to attack certain military objectives in Germany.
3. Mines were to be laid in the Rhine (Operation 'Royal Marines').

[21] Cab 65/12 71(40)6, 18 March. Cab 66/6 WP(40)101, 18 March.
[22] Cab 65/6 76(40)3, 27 March (and see also Cab 80/9 COS (40)279). Cab 66/6 WP(40)106, 26 March.

Anglo-French diplomatic requests for permission to enter Belgium were presented on 11 April, and supported by a personal telegram from Gamelin to King Leopold. Once again the Belgians refused.[23] Spaak replied that the Belgian Government might be prepared to consider the request more favourably if the Allies would agree to take up positions on the Albert Canal and the line of the Meuse and so perhaps prevent war being fought in the heart of the country. Anyway they were not sure an attack was coming and would only invite the Allies in when certain.

Despite continuing equivocation from Gamelin, the Supreme War Council decided firmly in favour of preventive or anticipatory action on 23 April. It was resolved that if the Germans invaded Holland the Allies should at once advance into Belgium irrespective of the attitude which the Belgian Government might adopt. The extent of the advance would depend on Belgium's attitude. The latter should not be approached in advance but a joint note should be prepared and handed to the Belgians when an act of aggression took place.[24]

Thus the frustrations of the Phoney War, humiliating failure in Norway, and the reluctance of small nations to offer themselves as a battlefield caused the Allies to adopt a highly questionable policy towards Belgium. Although the eventual result was bad enough, it was a small mercy that Hitler attacked Holland and Belgium simultaneously. Otherwise there might well have ensued the unedifying spectacle of the Allies fighting their way through the territory of one small neutral in an effort to bring assistance to another.

In harmony with their policy of neutrality the Belgians continued to decline all invitations to staff conversations with the Allies thoughout the period of the Phoney War. France and Britain gleaned a good deal of military information through their attachés but both felt some resentment at the lack of more direct co-operation. To judge from his diary notes, General Van Overstraeten's main themes in his dealings with the Allies in the spring of 1940 were firstly Belgium's claim to the exclusive use of the city of Brussels in the event of war and, second, his vain attempts to persuade the Allies to agree to advance beyond the line of the Dyle. Despite his sarcastic remarks to Colonels Hautcoeur and Blake to the effect that the Belgian army would be slaughtered east of the Dyle while the Allies were slowly taking up their positions, Van Overstraeten realized that Antwerp-Namur constituted the true battle line and the Albert Canal only provided a covering line.[25]

The inadequacy of Anglo-French liaison with the Low Countries is suggested by a Foreign Office paper dated 26 March. As regards Belgium, questions had been submitted through a special contact and some replies had been received (Van Overstraeten, for example, had given Colonel Blake aerial photographs of the Albert Canal to assist RAF targeting and had been

[23] Cab 65/12 90(40)2, 12 April. Cab 66/7 WP(40)126, 11 April. Shirer pp. 677-8. *Les Relations Militaires* pp. 126-8.
[24] Cab 66/7 WP(40)136, 23 April, see also *ibid* 143, 3 May. *Ironside Diaries* pp. 233-6, 279.
[25] Overstraeten pp. 506-33 *passim*.

thanked by the Chief of Air Staff). 'Franco-Belgian contacts are suspected', the paper continued artlessly, 'but we have no official knowledge of their nature and scope.' Questions had also been submitted to the Netherlands and although no replies had yet been received the atmosphere was said to be 'not unfavourable'.[26]

On 1 April the CIGS met Colonel Blake at Arras and was told that the Belgians would not deal with the French as they resented being treated as inferiors. Van Overstraeten had told Blake that he was convinced the French would never come past the Namur-Wavre-Antwerp line and so he would not deal with them. Ironside instructed Blake to say that he and Gamelin were agreed that the Allies would have to be established on the Dyle line before they could think of going any further.[27]

Thus, although the King of the Belgians and his chief military adviser were satisfied that they were supplying as much information as their potential allies needed, the situation appeared far less satisfactory from the Anglo-French point of view. Fortunately the British were allowed to obtain some of the detailed information they needed (such as the location of Belgian anti-tank obstacles, arrangements for the defence of the Meuse bridges, siting of engineer stores behind the Dyle) through secret visits by officers in civilian clothes. One of these, the Commander of I Corps Artillery (CCRA), the late Major-General F. H. N. Davidson, has left an account of his mission to Belgium in March 1940.[28]

On General Dill's instructions he changed into mufti at the Embassy in Paris, received a civilian passport, and travelled to Brussels by train on the pretext of delivering a diplomatic bag. He then spent three days touring the Dyle position mostly in the military attaché's car—'there could of course be no question of our walking about with opened maps or anything like that'. He found that the Dyle line was far from being a well-prepared defensive position: there were only a few small and rather conspicuous concrete pill-boxes; also some stretches of steel anti-tank fencing. As a gunner, Davidson put the visit to good use by noting all the areas suitable for battery positions and observation posts to serve them. He and Blake also discovered several important errors on their maps, including a new main road by-passing Brussels which 2 Division would use in the withdrawal in May. By the end of the visit Davidson says he knew every inch of the terrain—defences, roads, lakes, forests and a complete artillery layout. This and similar clandestine visits were doubtless of great value to the BEF, yet even so there remained a great amount of ignorance on the parts of the British and French as to Belgian operational plans, defensive obstacles and other military installations.[29]

[26] *Ibid*, p. 519. Cab 66/6 WP(40)106.
[27] *Ironside Diaries* p. 241.
[28] Major-General F. H. N. Davidson 'My Mission to Belgium, 1940' in *RUSI Journal* December 1969, pp. 80-2. See also Ellis p. 24.
[29] However, in fairness to the Belgians, it should be stressed that a great deal of Allied ignorance

It is pointless to speculate to what extent these uncertainties could have been removed by official staff talks: the fact is that some of these problems (such as the use of the roads on the outskirts of Brussels) would lead to serious friction between the Allies and the Belgians at the very outset of the campaign.

With the wisdom of hindsight it is all too easy to perceive the weakness of the Allied position on the Western Front at the beginning of May 1940. Despite an impressive variety of accumulated intelligence reports, Gamelin and his subordinates had signally failed to deduce the true intentions of the German plan, but continued to expect a head-on confrontation in Belgium. Provided his troops had time to occupy the defensive position along the Dyle, Gamelin was reasonably confident of stemming the German flood. In reality this forward move, like the headlong offensive into Lorraine in August 1914, would play straight into the enemy's hands. The Allies would also be handicapped from the start by an incredibly cumbersome command and staff structure; by inadequate provision of liaison officers between the national contingents; and by poor communications in the political as well as in the military sphere. As if this was not enough, personal relations between the senior French generals, particularly Gamelin and Georges, were extremely strained, and the former was well aware that his Prime Minister wished to have him dismissed. Lastly, though of course this does not exhaust the Allies' problems and disadvantages, military arrangements with the Belgians—not to speak of the Dutch—left much to be desired; while mutual incomprehension of the other's viewpoint over such episodes as the false alarms in November, January and April had created a fund of ill-will and prejudice which would be speedily drawn upon when things began to go wrong. King Leopold's policy during this nerve-racking period seems, on the whole, realistic but General Van Overstraeten had done much to deserve the reputation of 'evil genius' with the senior French and British commanders long before the need arose for active co-operation on the field of battle.

Nevertheless the Allied commanders maintained a confident demeanour as the likely period for a German spring offensive approached. On 31 March Gamelin told Ironside he was puzzled by German inaction (this was of course just before Scandinavia was overrun), for he had expected to be attacked. Gamelin actually hoped that the Germans would attack and remained confident in the morale and fighting spirit of the French Army. Ironside recorded in the privacy of his diary that he had a low opinion of the German generals and their staff work; an attack on the Western Front would be a terrible gamble for them.[30]

---

of Belgium was due to faulty intelligence work, poor liaison between British and French headquarters, and excessive secrecy. Marc Bloch, for example, records that 'GHQ had doled out to us very vague and often erroneous particulars about the position, the capacity, and the contents of the various (fuel) dumps... We had no idea how the fuel-supply service in the Belgian Army was organized...' Marc Bloch *Strange Defeat* (New York, Norton, 1968) p. 82ff.
[30] *Ironside Diaries* p. 241.

3

The Isolation of the
Allied Armies in Belgium
10-21 May 1940

In the history of warfare few campaigns between great and approximately equal powers have been decided so swiftly and conclusively as the German conquest of Western Europe in May and June 1940. Within five days of the opening of the campaign on 10 May, the Allied defences had been breached beyond repair, Paris appeared defenceless and the French Prime Minister was already talking of defeat. By 20 May the Allied forces north of the Somme had been cut off from the main French forces, and though a large proportion of the troops escaped via Dunkirk, most of their weapons and equipment were lost. Thus weakened, deprived of her allies on land, and attacked in the rear by Italy, France—widely regarded hitherto as the foremost military power—ignominiously sought peace on 22 June.

In the light of Germany's previous and subsequent application of the novel techniques of *blitzkrieg* it was easy—and perhaps consoling from the generals' viewpoint—to believe that France and her allies had been victims of overwhelming military might. Alternatively some historians refused to accept as adequate the military explanations of defeat and sought more profound causes in French political, social and economic life.[1] Gradually, however, the neat black and white caricature became blurred and grey as more information became available: it was discovered for example, that there had been fumblings, hesitations and errors on the German side; indeed that some German generals had been astonished by the speed and magnitude of their victory. Not least important, sober post-war analysis indicated increasingly that Germany had in most respects not enjoyed—except in the air—any marked qualitative or numerical superiority. This disquieting revelation served to focus attention once more on the victor's superior strategic doctrine, operational skills and command system. Some excellent recent studies of the campaign have appropriately examined in great detail the German

---

[1] See for example Marc Bloch *Strange Defeat* especially Chapter 3 'A Frenchman examines his conscience'.

breakthrough on the Meuse in the Sedan area, which the French were never able to check.[2]

This aspect of the campaign has been exhaustively studied from all sides; but less attention has been paid to the political and strategic problems of the BEF, sandwiched as it was between French and Belgians in the North-Eastern Group of Armies. These problems, which influenced not only the immediate military situation but also long-term strategy and post-war national attitudes, are sufficiently interesting to merit the spotlight, particularly as it has hitherto been extremely difficult to discuss them with a reasonable degree of objectivity.

For most of the participants, even those who defied the regulations by keeping diaries, the events of May 1940 were apt in retrospect to seem confused and condensed. Constant movement, lack of sleep, harrowing sights and depressing prospects all served to thicken the usual 'fog of war'. Thus some diarists admit that their chronology is uncertain, while the very wealth of evidence has created a veritable minefield of conflicting testimony for the unwary historian. As the late Guy Chapman, one of the most thorough and careful students of the campaign, remarked, 'There are great difficulties as to facts about these days... The only thing that emerges from most writings is that neither French nor British ever informed the other of what they were intending to do and doing'.[3]

The historian nevertheless has a duty to impose order where, for the actors, there was often only muddle and chaos. Even in the first eleven days of active operations, from 10 to 21 May, three phases may be discerned:

1. The advance to and occupation of the Dyle line when Gamelin's plan seemed to be working fairly well.
2. Appreciation of the repercussions of the disaster to the south by 15 May and leisurely withdrawal to the Escaut (16-19 May).
3. Changes in the French High Command and the attempt to reorganize for a counter-attack (19-21 May).

Two salient points emerge from an examination of these eleven days: first neither the French nor the British political and military leaders—not even Churchill—were fully able to grasp the tempo at which events were happening in the field; and, secondly, the cumbersome and illogical Allied command system virtually ceased to function under the unexpected strain it had to bear. Sharply differing national preoccupations and mutual suspicions, which had never been successfully subordinated to the needs of the alliance,

---

[2] For the balance of forces in May 1940 see R. H. S. Stolfi 'Equipment for Victory in France in 1940' in *History*, February 1970, pp. 1-20, and Shirer *op. cit.*, pp. 696-700. On French military doctrine see R. A. Doughty *The Seeds of Disaster* (Hamden, C: Archon Books, 1985). Recent studies which examine the German breakthrough on the Meuse in detail include A. Goutard *1940: La Guerre des occasions perdues* (1956); Alistair Horne *To Lose a Battle* (1969) and Guy Chapman *Why France Collapsed* (1968).

[3] Chapman, *op. cit.*, p. 365.

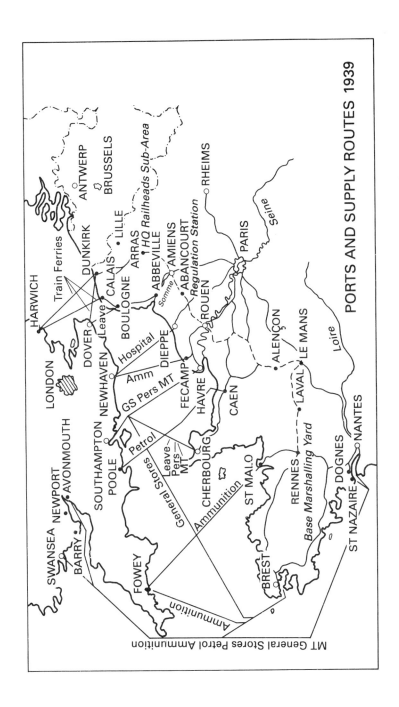

PORTS AND SUPPLY ROUTES 1939

quickly surfaced when things began to go wrong and weighted the odds still further against a military recovery.

When the Germans attacked Holland, Belgium and Luxembourg in the early hours of 10 May, 1940, Allied assistance was called for and Gamelin implemented Plan D. On the left wing, Giraud's 7 Army swiftly advanced into Holland, some units going as far east as Breda and Tilburg, but, as critics had feared, a precipitate Dutch withdrawal deprived it of a clear mission. Shaken by dive bombing and running short of ammunition 7 Army withdrew even more speedily on 13 and 14 May with little accomplished.

On the whole the advance of the main French and British forces to the Dyle line by 12 May went remarkably smoothly. In particular there was so little harassment from the air that one or two diarists speculated (correctly) that the enemy's restraint might be deliberate. Nevertheless the strong anti-Belgian prejudices of some of the French and British generals found plenty to feed on. Not all the prejudice was ill-founded and there were faults on both sides: it was tragic, however, that mutual understanding and tolerance were soured at the very outset of the campaign before the alliance was called upon to face really stern tests.

The Belgians had certainly made it clear beforehand that they intended to retain sole use of the roads through Brussels but the British, particularly Montgomery's 3 Division, could hardly avoid the outskirts of the capital in advancing to garrison Louvain. On 13 May Sir Roger Keyes, who had recently returned to Belgium as Churchill's representative, protested when the King and Van Overstraeten complained that British troops were using Brussels. He pointed out that Van Overstraeten had promised to make additional bridges available but had not supplied the British military attaché with the relevant information. When Montgomery's division arrived at Louvain in the dark on 11 May they found the Belgian 10 Division in occupation and were fired upon in the belief that they were German parachutists. The Belgian general refused to yield but Montgomery eventually got his way in characteristically impish style. According to Montgomery, he placed himself under the Belgian's orders on the correct assumption that the latter would pull out as soon as the Germans came within artillery range and began shelling. In the meantime his Corps commander, Lieutenant General Sir Alan Brooke, sought to put the matter right in an interview with King Leopold. His note on the meeting is very revealing on Anglo-Belgian mistrust:

As I came in I saw no one else in the room, and Roger Keyes withdrew and left me alone with the King. I explained to him my difficulties... in English. I found him charming to talk to, and felt that I was making progress... when I suddenly heard a voice speaking in French from behind my right. On turning round I found an officer there who did not introduce himself to me but went on speaking in French to the King. His contention was that the Belgian Division could not be moved, that the whole of the BEF should be stepped farther south and be entirely clear of Brussels. I then turned on him in French and told him that he was not putting the full case before the King, since he had not mentioned that the 10th Belgian Division was on the wrong side of the Gamelin Line. He then turned to me, and said: 'Oh! do you speak French?' I assured him that I did, and that I happened to have been born in France. By that time he had interposed himself between me and the King. I therefore walked round him and resumed my conversation with the King in English.

This individual then came round again and placed himself between me and the King, and the King withdrew to the window. I could not very well force my presence a third time on the King, and I therefore discussed the matter with this individual whom I assumed must be the Chief of Staff (it was in fact Van Overstraeten). I found that arguing with him was sheer waste of time; he was not familiar with the dispositions of the BEF, and seemed to care little about them. Most of his suggestions were fantastic.

I left the Belgian GHQ with many misgivings in my heart. As I motored back to Brussels I wondered whether the Belgians would turn out to be no better than the French. My left flank was to rest on the Belgian Army; these thoughts were consequently most disconcerting . . .[4]

The Allies had more serious grounds for complaint on the subject of the Belgian anti-tank defences along the Dyle and southwards to cover the riverless gap betwen Wavre and Namur. Only a few days before the advance began, GHQ was alarmed to discover that the Belgians had sited their anti-tank defences (known as the *de Cointet* obstacle) several miles east of the Dyle on the line Namur-Perwez; furthermore it was incomplete. The French I Army found similar gaps on their sector.[5]

It was however, on the crucial question of the Belgian ability to hold up the attacker on their eastern frontier—and particularly the Albert Canal— that even GHQ's estimate of the worst possible case proved insufficiently pessimistic. In a brilliant tactical coup German gliders landed troops on the 'impregnable' fortress of Eben Emael in advance of the main attack and captured it within twenty-four hours. The Germans, moreover, established bridgeheads across the Albert Canal before the leading British unit, the 12th Lancers, had reached the Dyle. Further south the Belgian Chasseurs Ardennais, following the orders of their High Command, withdrew behind the Meuse without fighting after carrying out demolitions. These, and other incidents, caused the BEF's Chief of Staff to write in exasperation on 13 May: 'All the Belgians seem to be in a panic, from the higher command downwards. What an ally!' Three days later Daladier muttered despairingly to Paul Baudouin 'The mistake, the unpardonable mistake, was to send so many men into Belgium'. In retrospect Churchill recorded, more moderately, that the Belgian failure to hold their eastern frontiers for at least several days had fulfilled the apprehensions of the Chiefs of Staff by exposing

---

[4] For the Belgian attitude to the Allies' use of Brussels see Overstraeten pp. 483, 488, 503-10, 526-7, 534-5; Montgomery *The Memoirs of Field Marshal Montgomery* (Fontana paperback edition) p. 60; Arthur Bryant *The Turn of the Tide 1939-1943* (Alanbrooke Diaries) (Collins, 1957) pp. 93-7, 101. Admiral Sir Roger Keyes *Diary of the Belgian Campaign, May, 1940* (henceforth referred to as *Keyes Diary*) entry for 13 May. See also Paul Halpern (ed) *The Keyes Papers* Vol. III (Allen & Unwin, 1981) pp. 44-74.

[5] *Pownall Diaries* pp. 309-10, Chapman p. 105, Colville p. 181.

the British and French divisions to an encounter battle in unprepared positions.[6]

There was nevertheless a brief reassuring lull on the Dyle front before the terrible news of the Ardennes breakthrough filtered through. By 11 May the Allied cavalry and light armoured units were pushing a covering screen east of the Dyle and Meuse while the artillery and infantry moved up more slowly by road and rail. General Billotte's Army Group I (French 7 and 1 Armies and the BEF) contained thirty divisions with which to hold a front of about fifty-five miles without counting the Belgian army (estimated at between eighteen and twenty-two divisions). Moreover, Billotte's army contained the bulk of France's armoured forces, including all three light armoured divisions and two out of three heavy armoured divisions. It was markedly superior in numbers, guns and armour to Reichenau's opposing 6 Army. Thus it seemed briefly that Gamelin's gamble on Plan D would be justified and the Germans held in eastern Belgium. General Ironside noted in his diary on 11 May that the slow pace of the German advance should enable the Allies to fortify the Dyle line. He expected a long, hard battle to continue throughout the summer, but remained confident that the advantage lay with the Allies. According to Ironside, the British Chief of Air Staff believed the German objective was to secure Holland as a base from which to bomb Britain; Ironside was not yet prepared to dismiss the idea.[7]

The best that can be said for the French command system is that it might just have sufficed for a static siege war like that of 1914-1918. As already explained, Gamelin had manifested his dislike of responsibility by dissipating his authority amongst three widely separated headquarters: he himself remained at Vinçennes, Georges at La Ferté some thirty-five miles to the east near which, at Montry, was situated GQG under the Chief of Staff, General Doumenc. To complicate matters, Georges spent much of his time at a personal command post—a house called Les Bondons just outside La Ferté, while the bureaux—or staff sections—were divided between the three headquarters. As if this was not confused enough, communications were archaic. Surprisingly there was no teletype service between the headquarters or from them to the armies in the field. Telephone services were inefficient even under peacetime conditions and telegrams took a long time to reach their destinations. Gamelin's command post at Vinçennes lacked a radio or, as one of his aides complained, even carrier pigeons. In short, the C-in-C was isolated from the first day of the battle, his headquarters, in the metaphor of one staff officer, 'a submarine without a periscope'. How then did the French higher commanders communicate with each other? Principally by a

[6] Colville p. 191, Shirer p. 716, *Pownall Diaries* pp. 314-15, Baudouin p. 32, Winston S. Churchill *The Second World War* Vol 2 (Cassell, 1949), p. 26 (henceforth referred to as Churchill). E. Wanty 'Improvisation de la liaison belgo-britannique du 10 mai au 18 mai 1940' in *Revue d'histoire de la deuxième guerre mondiale* January 1964, pp. 29-50.
[7] Shirer p. 694. *Ironside Diaries* pp. 302-6.

regular procession of motor-cyclists, which in war conditions all too frequently met with accidents; or by personal visits which at the very least were tiring and time consuming.

On a slightly lower level, at 1 Army headquarters the distinguished historian and veteran of the First World War, Marc Bloch, noted that a number of alarming cracks had developed in the military fabric in the months before May 1940: 'One of them was the wholly inadequate organization of our communications'. Bloch also had severe strictures to make on French 1 Army's intelligence organization; only too often 1 Army had no idea where its own corps were situated, and on one important occasion he personally was told they had no idea of the whereabouts of Lord Gort's headquarters. In a long and moving passage on the failure of Allied liaison, Bloch concluded that:

> Co-operation could have been proof against the difficulties of the time only if it had been firmly based earlier. A genuine alliance is something that has to be worked at all the time. It is not enough to have it set down on paper. It must draw the breath of life from a multiplicity of daily contacts which, taken together, knit the two parties into a single whole.[8]

Bloch was also admirably astringent on the fact that historians should focus their attention on men rather than functions: 'The errors of the High Command were, fundamentally, the errors of a specific group of human beings'. Although some of the junior staff offices of 1 Army emerged well from the disaster the commander, General Blanchard, appeared to be stunned by events beyond his control. Bloch recalls an hour in his presence during which he sat in tragic immobility 'saying nothing, doing nothing, but just gazing at the map spread on the table between us...' André Beaufre, also then a junior staff officer at GQG, has described the 'fiction flood' which poured in from Army headquarters in the opening days of the campaign and which was relayed hourly to Gamelin by dispatch rider. In the early hours of 14 May he accompanied his chief, General Doumenc, to Georges' command post:

> The atmosphere was that of a family in which there had just been a death. Georges got up quickly and came to Doumenc. He was terribly pale. 'Our front has been broken at Sedan! There has been a collapse...' He flung himself into a chair and burst into tears.
> He was the first man I had seen weep on this campaign. Alas, there were to be others. It made a terrible impression on me.
> Doumenc, taken aback by this greeting, reacted immediately. 'General, this is war and in war things like this are bound to happen!' Then Georges, still pale, explained: following terrible bombardment from the air the two inferior divisions had taken to their heels. 10 Corps signalled that the position was penetrated and that German tanks had arrived in Bulson at about midnight. Here there was another flood of tears. Everyone else remained silent, shattered by what had happened.
> 'Well, General,' said Doumenc, 'all wars have their routs. Let us look at the map and see what can be done.' He spoke firmly in these darkened surroundings and it made me feel better.

8 Shirer pp. 706-8. Bloch pp. 58, 64-8, 77-81.

Major A. O. Archdale, British liaison officer at Billotte's headquarters, describes a similar scene with staff officers weeping on 15 May.[9]

It would be wrong to make invidious comparisons with British GHQ where fewer tears and personal breakdowns were witnessed. After all, Lord Gort and his generals had less scope for illusions about the training and equipment of their ten active divisions; but more important they were a comparatively small cog in the French war machine and it was not their country which was being overrun for the second time within memory. Indeed, Lord Gort is equally open to criticism in the arrangement of his command system but rather for the opposite reason to Gamelin: he was essentially a brave fighting soldier who longed to take part in offensive action at the front, rather than wait for the enemy to take the initiative. One Frenchman's description of him as 'a jovial battalion commander', while unfair, conveyed a good deal of truth about Gort's character.[10]

Ironically Gort's dilemma was exacerbated by the fact that he lacked an equivalent of Georges who would assume day to day command of the divisions in the field. Unfortunately when the blow fell, Gort was still filling the dual role of C-in-C of a national contingent responsible to the British Government, and field commander of a subordinate force within the French command structure (albeit with right of appeal). Gort intended to relinquish the latter function to two army commanders when IV Corps was formed later in the summer.

Gort's solution was somewhat similar to Rommel's personal command method in North Africa later in the war: both had their merits as well as short-comings but in Gort's case the latter were more evident. Immediately operations began, Gort set off with a small body of staff officers, including his Chief of Staff, to a pre-arranged command post at Wahagnies, ten miles south of Lille. He left behind at Arras some two hundred and fifty officers and clerks, including the majority of his Operations and Intelligence staff. Gort's biographer has described this separation of the commander from his main GHQ as 'an administrative disaster'. As communications deteriorated due to the German advance, and Gort was frequently compelled to move his command post, the link between Gort and the nucleus of his staff was virtually severed. Depletion of the Intelligence Branch at GHQ had particularly serious consequences. 'Information received direct at GHQ often failed to pass from the Intelligence Staff at the Command Post to formations at the front in time to be of use to them, while much of the information which divisions at the front sent into the Command Post was never passed back to

[9] Bloch pp. 27-8. A. Beaufre *1940: the Fall of France* (Cassell, 1967) pp. 18-23. Major A. O. Archdale *Liaison with the 1st Group of French Armies October 1939-May 1940* (henceforth referred to as *Archdale Diary*), entry for 15 May.

[10] Sir John Kennedy gives an amusing example of Gort's obsession with detail. At a Commander-in-Chief's conference in France in November 1939, the first question Gort raised was whether a tin hat, when it was not on a man's head, should be worn on the left shoulder or the right. Kennedy *The Business of War* (Hutchinson, 1957) p. 36.

General Headquarters at Arras'. To anticipate a little, when, on 17 May, Gort feared that the breakthrough on the Meuse might expose a gap on the right rear of the BEF, he formed a scratch force under Major General F. N. Mason-Macfarlane, his Director of Military Intelligence, thus depriving himself of a key staff officer. As the official historian remarks with characteristic under emphasis 'the necessity for this step may perhaps be questioned', and adds 'almost certainly it would have been wiser not to take General Mason-Macfarlane and a senior staff officer (Lieutenant Colonel Gerald Templer) from the work of Intelligence at Command Post'. General Montgomery, who had a low opinion of the BEF's staff work and training generally, bluntly called this 'an amazing decision'. In his forthright opinion the staff plan was 'amateur and lacked the professional touch'. He concluded that British and French control of the forces available on 10 May was a 'complete dog's breakfast' for which Gamelin primarily stood responsible, but Gort and his Chief of Staff were also implicated.[11]

A further link in the already long Allied chain of command was forged as the result of a conference at the Château Casteau near Mons on 12 May. The Belgian policy of neutrality had hitherto made it impossible for their Army to be given a definite place in the Allied chain of command, and, moreover, General Georges had by now decided that his headquarters were too far away for him to control personally the two French armies (1 and 7), the BEF and the Belgian army on the north-eastern front. King Leopold and General Pownall (representing Gort) agreed to accept General Billotte as co-ordinator. Gamelin gives cogent reasons for his disapproval of this 'abdictation' of responsibility by Georges, but as usual he did not interfere. To change the metaphor, the command structure was only further fragmented. Billotte, commanding 1 Army Group, was not personally suitable for this extremely difficult assignment.[12]

Major Archdale, whose diary charts the decline at Billotte's headquarters, had been unfavourably impressed during the winter months by the obsession with desk work to the exclusion of all other normal activities. 'This frenzy of paper output and lack of physical and mental relaxation', he wrote, 'resulted without any doubt in staleness and nerve strain where none should have existed, and in a want of liaison with the Armies'. On 13 May, when Gort sent a message to Billotte that he was prepared to carry out his orders, Billotte seemed to Archdale to be at his best, 'suave and courteous, and apparently untroubled by the rapidly deteriorating news from the 9 Army'. This was a delusion. On the following day, when he witnessed a meeting between Billotte and Giraud—both over six feet tall and massively built—he thought that Giraud brought an atmosphere of command and confidence 'to which we were already strangers at our HQ'.

---

[11] Colville pp. 190-1, 195, 199. Ellis pp. 64-5, Montgomery pp. 56-7.
[12] Ellis p. 42. *Pownall Diaries* pp. 311-13. Gamelin *Servir I* pp. 318-21. Shirer pp. 710-11.

These forebodings proved justified by Billotte's indecisiveness and defeatism in the critical days that followed. He failed to issue firm directives and never won the confidence of the commanders whose armies he was supposed to control.[13]

By 14 May Billotte had definite information about the collapse of 9 Army so that the danger of his Army Group being cut off must have occurred to him. Yet two more days passed before he issued instructions to withdraw, and even then the pace was to be leisurely. General Prioux, commanding the Cavalry Corps, and one of the few generals to emerge from the defeat with credit, had already advised, on 11 May, that in view of the unprepared defences on the Dyle and the rapid enemy breaching of the Albert Canal, the main Allied forces should be halted at or return to the Scheldt (ie, the original Plan E). Prioux was supported by Blanchard but Billotte decided it was too late to change Gamelin's orders. Gamelin of course retained the final military responsibility and his will appeared to be paralysed. According to Paul Baudouin, the Prime Minister, Reynaud was opposed to any advance into Belgium but Daladier told him in effect to leave Gamelin alone. On 14 May Reynaud again enquired if the armies, still east of Brussels, had been ordered to fall back, but the reply was in the negative. Baudouin adds 'We felt that the situation had suddenly become tragic'.[14]

After a request from Gort for definite orders early on 16 May, Billotte issued instructions that the Allies would retire in the following stages to the Scheldt: night of 16-17 May to the River Senne; night of 17-18 to the River Dendre; night of 18-19 to the River Escaut (Scheldt). The Belgians were naturally adverse to abandoning Louvain and Brussels, particularly as up to then the Dyle line had withstood German pressure. A car accident involving the head of the British military mission at Belgian headquarters (General Needham) meant that they were slow to learn that the British on their right flank proposed to retreat that evening, 16 May. This was just one—and by no means the worst—of many misunderstandings or failures to pass on orders which soured Anglo-French-Belgian relations during the retreat. Between 16 and 19 May the withdrawal plan was complicated by the issue of contradictory orders from General Georges and by the vacillation of Billotte, who was under pressure from Blanchard (parts of whose 1 Army were admittedly heavily engaged) either to delay the withdrawal owing to the exhaustion of his troops, or to hurry it on owing to the pressure on his front. On the morning of 18 May, for example, Gort agreed to stay one extra night on the Dendre (ie 18-19 May) if German pressure was not too great and liaison was maintained on both his flanks. Later in the day Billotte changed his mind and said the move must take place that night after all. Gort replied that he could not change his plans again and would look after his own

---

[13] *Archdale Diary* p. 2 and entries for 10 May, 13 and 14 May. Colville p. 195.
[14] Chapman p. 101. Shirer p. 713. Baudouin pp. 28-30. Bloch. p. 41.

flanks. Strong British rearguards remained on the Dendre until the morning of the 19th.[15]

It needs to be emphasized that after heavy fighting all along the Dyle line on 15 May, the only part of the British front to be severely tested on the 16th was Louvain, tenaciously defended by Montgomery's 3 Division. Thereafter the BEF was not vigorously pursued in its retreat to the Escaut, particularly in comparison with parts of 1 French Army on its right. Von Bock, commanding Army Group B, had ordered a 'prepared attack' for the 17th to pierce the Wavre-Namur front, but by this time the British were back on the Senne. Ironside accurately recorded on 18 May that the BEF seemed to have withdrawn to the Dendre without being hurried in any way, and three days later Pownall appreciated that the BEF had still only encountered the vanguard of the Army Group B. That same day (21 May) Ironside reported to the Prime Minister that the BEF had so far suffered only about 500 battle casualties.[16]

With the benefit of hindsight it is easy to see that Billotte should have withdrawn to the frontier more quickly, first to avoid being cut off by the German thrust along the Somme valley and second to prepare a counter-offensive to interrupt that thrust. However, given the deplorable state of Allied intelligence, a ruthless order was required from Gamelin (directly or via Georges) and in this he failed completely. Billotte was preoccupied by the problems of getting three mutually suspicious national contingents to withdraw in harmony; liaison on all sides was poor; and the Belgians very naturally were loath to abandon the heart of their country when undefeated simply to conform with their allies. Already by 18 May it was becoming doubtful whether 1 Army Group possessed the political and military cohesion to fight its way either south to the Somme or south-west towards Amiens.

Lord Gort's anxiety during the retreat to the Escaut was increased by the feeling that the significance of the German breakthrough was not fully understood in London. He was right. Churchill has candidly admitted that when Reynaud telephoned early in the morning on the 15 May to announce 'We are beaten; we have lost the battle', he could not believe it. Surely, he interjected, the Germans would soon have to halt for supplies and then would be the time to counter-attack as Foch had done in March 1918? Churchill adds that the idea of the line being broken, even on a wide front, did not convey to his mind the appalling consequences that would ensue.

Not having access to official information for so many years, I did not comprehend the violence of the revolution effected since the last war by the incursion of a mass of fast-moving

---

[15] *Archdale Diary* entries for 15, 16 and 18 May. Ellis pp. 59-67. *Pownall Diaries* pp. 318-19. Colville pp. 200, 202.
[16] Ellis p. 62. *Pownall Diaries* p. 327. *Ironside Diaries* p. 318. Churchill p. 55. Cab 65/7 132(40), 21 May.

heavy armour. I knew about it, but it had not altered my inward convictions as it should have done. There was nothing I could have done if it had.

Churchill has left an inimitable description of his visit to Paris on 16 May with Dill and Ismay. Throughout his meeting with the French political and military leaders everyone remained standing. Utter dejection was written on every face. After Gamelin had unemotionally, as though giving an academic lecture, described the disaster for about five minutes, pointing out that the Germans could either make for Abbeville or Paris, Churchill burst out in his indifferent French: 'Où est la masse de manoeuvre?', to which Gamelin replied with a shake of the head and a shrug: 'Aucune'.*

> There was another long pause. Outside in the garden of the Quai d'Orsay clouds of smoke arose from large bonfires, and I saw from the window venerable officials pushing wheel-barrows of archives on to them. Already therefore the evacuation of Paris was being prepared.

What should be done? Reynaud was later to allege that Churchill urged that there should be no withdrawal of the northern armies, that on the contrary they should counter-attack. Churchill agrees that this fairly represented his mood but that he did not intend to recommend any particular military measures. (Cadogan noted that before leaving for France Churchill had been furious when Dill explained the plans for withdrawal in Belgium.) Clearly at that stage he was not aware of the urgent need for the northern armies to retreat if they were to avoid being encircled. The only immediate step which the Prime Minister could take to hearten the French was to send out another six fighter squadrons to add to the four already promised. A modest contribution to the alliance but in the opinion of one distinguished historian 'extravagant waste'. What *did* strike Churchill and everyone else present was Gamelin's utter incapacity to deal with the crisis. Reynaud decided to bring the seventy-three-year-old Weygand back from Syria to take over the supreme command.[17]

Ironside's diary for these days (16-18 May) reveals that he quickly grasped the nature of the dilemma which would soon confront Gort. The best strategic move for the BEF, in his view, was south or south-west to maintain its communications through Amiens and to link up with the main French forces, but this would surely entail abandoning the Belgians. The alternative, which he was loath to contemplate, was a withdrawal north to the Channel ports. This would mean the abandonment of Britain's principal ally and the almost certain loss of the BEF's heavy weapons and equipment. On 17 May Ironside described evacuation from the Channel ports as 'an impossible proposition' but his editors note that on that day (two days *before* Gort proposed the same precautions) he suggested to the Admiralty that all small

---

* Gamelin may have said 'Anywhere', but the effect was the same.
[17] Churchill pp. 38-44. *Cadogan Diaries* p. 284. Baudouin pp. 32-3. Chapman p. 172.

vessels should be collected and organized with a view to evacuating the men of the BEF if the worst should happen.[18] Ironside's preferred solution of a break-out to the south-west was still just about a practical possibility on 19 May, but it was becoming hourly more hazardous. The replacement of Gamelin by Weygand and Billotte's chronic indecision caused the chance to be missed, and Gort began to harden in the view that there was no way out to the south for the BEF.

The consideration which probably did most to condition Gort's mind before Ironside arrived at his headquarters early on the morning of 20 May, was the conviction that the BEF's fate could not be safely entrusted to the French commanders in 1 Army Group, particularly Billotte.

By 18 May Major Archdale had come to the conclusion that Billotte's inability to improvise and act might imperil the BEF, and he determined to warn Gort of this 'malignant inaction'. Not only Billotte himself, but also his Chief of Staff, Colonel Humbert, had broken down and the younger members of the staff poured out to the British officer their disgust and contempt at the supine futility of their commander and higher staff. Archdale saw Pownall at Wahagnies on 18 May, but the British Chief of Staff assured him that the French would soon recover from their fatigue and show more fight; he hinted that Archdale himself was over-tired and too much influenced by his propinquity to the French. Billotte however soon confirmed Archdale in his pessimism. The French commander spread out a map of the German order of battle with red circles indicating the armoured divisions in front of the Allied line and counted slowly 'Un panzer, deux panzers' and so on up to 'huit panzers' adding 'et contre ceux-la je ne peux rien faire'. Archdale decided the only hope was to arrange a meeting between the despondent Billotte and the boisterous, offensive-minded Gort. It took place at 11.00 pm that same evening at Gort's headquarters. To Gort's cheerful enquiry 'Eh bien! mon Général, qu'est-ce que vous avez à me dire?', Billotte swiftly made it clear that he had no plan, no reserves and little hope. On the way back to his headquarters (at Douai) he repeated constantly: 'Je suis crevé de fatigue, crevé de fatigue', and then pathetically, 'Et contre ces panzers je ne peux rien faire'.[19]

This meeting, and reports that came in on the morning of 19 May, suggested to GHQ that there was a complete void on the British right flank with only a disorganized mass of 'fag-ends' from 1 Army to fill it. There seemed no reason at all why at least two Panzer divisions should not appear on the British rear flank between Arras and Peronne, striking either west for Boulogne and Calais or north-west against the British flank. Pownall notes that after lunch the situation appeared brighter. There were not after all any Germans at 'X', 'Y' and 'Z' and 1 Army 'reappeared from somewhere'. The

[18] *Ironside Diaries* pp. 311-19. Ironside did not succumb to the anti-ally prejudices prevalent at GHQ, see *ibid* p. 313.
[19] *Archdale Diary* entry for 18 May.

evening, he remarked, ended tranquilly, 'But, my God what a morning!'[20] In the meantime he and Gort had made a move which had momentous consequences.

Pownall made two telephone calls (at 11.30 am and 1.30 pm) to his successor as Director of Military Operations at the War Office, Major General R. H. Dewing, and explained in camouflaged language that the BEF might be forced to withdraw. They were examining the possibility of a withdrawal in the direction of Dunkirk from where it might be possible to ship some troops home. An alternative withdrawal towards Bruges and Ostend (which Brooke favoured) was also being examined. Pownall stressed that they were in good heart and were definitely not going to withdraw at present, but only if the necessity were forced on them by the failure of the French to close the gap to the south. Pownall took the precaution of having his handwritten account of what he had said endorsed by Gort and two of the corps commanders, Brooke and Barker. Dewing had revealed himself out of touch ('he was singularly stupid and unhelpful') with German progress by suggesting that the BEF make for Boulogne.[21]

These telephone calls had two immediate and far-reaching effects.

First, the majority of the War Cabinet (and the CIGS, who was present) were displeased to hear that Gort was even contemplating a retreat to the Channel ports. Ironside was instructed to travel to France that night (19 May) to order Gort to move south-west and to force his way through all opposition in order to rejoin the main French forces. The Belgians were to be urged to conform to this movement or, alternatively, we would evacuate as many as possible of their troops from the Channel ports. The French Government would be informed of this resolution and General Dill (still Vice-Chief of the Imperial General Staff) would reinforce it in person by a four-day visit to General Georges. Churchill's account ends significantly: 'contacts even with Lord Gort were intermittent and difficult, but it was reported that only four days' supplies and ammunition for one battle were available.'

The second effect was, superficially, contradictory. On 20 May the War Cabinet agreed that even if the retreat to the Somme was carried out success-fully, some units might still need to be evacuated from the Channel ports. As a precautionary measure, therefore, Admiral Ramsay at Dover was instructed to assemble a large number of small vessels 'in readiness to proceed to ports and inlets on the French coast'.[22] Thus was initiated 'Operation Dynamo'. Britain was not at this time planning to abandon her

---

[20] *Pownall Diaries* pp. 321-3.

[21] *Ibid* pp. 323, 327-8. Bryant *The Turn of the Tide 1939-1943* p. 109.

[22] Churchill pp. 52-3. Chapman (p. 181) believes that the French monitoring service had probably picked up Pownall's conversation with the DMO at the War Office. This would account for Billotte's alarmist and unfortunately-timed telephone call to Georges that the British were thinking of retreating on Calais and Dunkirk. See Gamelin *Servir* III, pp. 431-2.

PLATE 1   Anti-tank traps laid
along the banks of a stream
in France. Autumn 1939.
(*Imperial War Museum*)

PLATE 2   Cameron Highlanders in
breastworks. 1st Btn. Queen's
Own Cameron Highlanders at Aix.
(*Imperial War Museum*)

PLATE 3   Mr Hore-Belisha watches troops building new bloc houses (1st day of tour at Cantine, near Douai).

PLATE 4 Mr Hore-Belisha with various British and French staff officers on high ground north of Tourcoing receiving explanations of the forward lines on the Belgian frontier (2nd day of tour) at Farquiscant. General Gort is in the foreground on the right. (*Imperial War Museum*)

PLATE 7 Left to right: Mr Winston Churchill; General Gort, Commander-in-Chief; Lieutenant General Pownall, CGS at Chateau de Couroy, near Avesnes. (*Imperial War Museum*)

PLATE 8   Anti-tank obstacle taken from Furm des Phillipaux. 779496 facing north in 2nd Lancashire Fusiliers, 4 Division area. 21.1.40. (*Imperial War Museum*)

PLATE 9   British tanks ready to join the Battle at Quesnoy, 30.5.40.
(*Imperial War Museum*)

PLATE 10 British troops halted by the wayside with their Bren carrier, while the ceaseless stream of Belgium refugees file past. (*Imperial War Museum*)

PLATE 11 Cavalry tanks on exercise, 31.3.40. (*Imperial War Museum*)

Continental allies but the early assembly of shipping—and the decision to evacuate some British units first—does go far to explain why so many more British than French troops were embarked at the end of May.

Meanwhile, after leaving the conduct of the battle to Georges for the first nine days, on 19 May—the very day on which he heard he was to be replaced by Weygand—Gamelin handed Georges a pencilled instruction (it was hardly an order) proposing a simultaneous counter attack from the north and south to cut off the German Panzer divisions from their supporting troops. Gamelin rightly concluded that 'it was a matter of hours', because the German spearhead was about to sever 1 Army Group's communication with Amiens and on the next day would reach the Channel coast at Abbeville. Gamelin's sense of urgency had clearly come too late from his own viewpoint and he departed imperturbable and self-righteous to the end. Georges was little better: Weygand described him as 'like a man who had received a violent blow in the stomach and finds it difficult to pull himself together again'. Weygand brought new vigour and confidence to the Government but in private he was not sanguine. Worst of all, he showed little more sense of urgency than his predecessor, whose vague plan for a counter-attack he postponed until he could examine the situation for himself. Baudouin notes ironically that after saying 'there was not a minute to lose' Weygand told him his immediate intention was to get a good night's sleep! Thus Ironside arrived in France to settle the role of the BEF on the very day, 20 May, that the latter's communications were severed and when the French Government was in the process of 'changing its horses in midstream'.[23]

Ironside reached Gort's command post at Wahagnies at 6.00 am on 20 May. He stated his opinion in support of the War Cabinet directive, that the only way for the BEF to break out of its encirclement was to march southwest towards Amiens. This, according to Sir John Slessor, who was present, caused a 'mild sensation'. Gort said this was impossible and refused to try. Seven of his nine divisions were in contact with the enemy on the Scheldt, and even if they could be disengaged their withdrawal would create a gap on his left between the BEF and the Belgians, through which the enemy would at once penetrate. The BEF had been marching and fighting for nine days without respite and was running short of ammunition. The main effort to plug the gap must be made by Weygand's forces from south of the Somme, but he would play his part by employing his two unengaged divisions at Arras the following day.

This order, the source of much confusion, had already been given to the commander, General Franklyn, and rather misleadingly became known as the 'Arras counter-attack'. The CIGS appears to have accepted Gort's

[23] Baudouin pp. 34-5. Chapman pp. 181-3. Shirer pp. 808-17. Besides the replacement of Gamelin by Weygand, Reynaud himself took over the Ministry of National Defence from Daladier (who returned to the Foreign Office), Marshal Pétain was appointed Deputy Prime Minister and Georges Mandel Minister of the Interior.

non possumus without further argument (though the latter was defying a Cabinet instruction) and, accompanied by Pownall, he went straight to see Billotte at Lens. His impressions of Billotte and Blanchard (who was also present) must surely have persuaded him that Gort's pessimism about the French was justified. Billotte was physically a big man, but Ironside was even larger. He admits that he lost his temper and shook the French general by the button of his tunic. Under Ironside's exhortation Billotte and Blanchard agreed to attack towards Cambrai on the morrow with two divisions.[24] If Ironside exaggerated in writing that there was absolutely nothing in front of them, the French generals and Gort probably erred in the other direction: Pownall's diary, quoted above, shows that the air was thick with false rumours of German units in the British rear areas. A determined march south-west on 21 May by 1 Army Group as a whole probably still stood a fair chance of breaking through. But confidence and mutual trust was lacking between the British and French commanders, quite apart from the separate problem of the Belgians.

The Belgian attitude was forcefully represented to Ironside at GHQ on 20 May by Sir Roger Keyes. The latter felt that the War Cabinet was quite out of touch with local conditions; an attack southwards carried out with the French in their present mood was almost certain to fail, and in any case was bound to lead to a break with the Belgians. Immediately after the meeting with Ironside, Keyes sent a cypher telegram to this effect to the Prime Minister, ending 'Am returning to Bruges and I do not propose to tell the Belgians that the BEF intends to desert them yet'.

After seeing King Leopold and his chief military advisers, Keyes dispatched another telegram to the Prime Minister with a copy to Gort. The King had pointed out that the Belgian Army existed solely for defence; it had neither tanks nor aircraft, and was not trained or equipped for offensive warfare. In the small part of Belgium still free, though flooded with refugees, he calculated that there was only sufficient food for a maximum of fourteen days. He did not expect the BEF to jeopardize its existence in order to keep in contact with the Belgian Army, but the British Government must realize what would happen if the BEF moved south: 'He (the King) realizes, of course, that such action would finally lead to the capitulation of the Belgian Army'. King Leopold was convinced that the BEF's best course would be to swing north-west at once, maintain close contact with the Belgians and establish a beach-head covering Dunkirk and the Belgian ports. The following day Keyes telephoned the Prime Minister from La Panne where the cable entered the sea, and vainly tried to convince him of the BEF's perilous

[24] *Ironside Diaries* pp. 320-3. *Pownall Diaries* pp. 323-4. Sir John Slessor *The Central Blue* pp. 288-9. Ellis pp. 83-5. While GHQ was convincing Ironside that the BEF could not break out southward, Dill was assuring Weygand that it would do so. Surprisingly Ironside does not seem to have informed the War Cabinet that Gort had convinced him that a southward attack was impossible, see Cab 65/7 132(40), 21 May.

situation. He got the impression that Churchill blamed him for suggesting that the order to Gort would, if carried out, inevitably lead to a break with the Belgians, though in fact Ironside had come to that conclusion first.[25] The significance of this exchange is that the opinions of Keyes and the King of the Belgians were now added to Gort's personal inclination against staking the fate of the BEF on a southward march. Like Keyes, GHQ felt that neither the War Office nor the Government appreciated the difficulty of their position.

The confusion prevailing at the command posts in 1 Army Group is nowhere better illustrated than in the British 'counter-attack' at Arras on 21 May. Gort's order given to General Franklyn on 20 May was to 'support the garrison in Arras and to block the roads south of Arras, thus cutting off the German communications from the east'. He was 'to occupy the line of the Scarpe on the east of Arras' and establish touch with the French. At that time there was no mention of a 'counter-attack' or of any more distant objective, nor was Franklyn told that the French would be participating in the operation. He was sure that Gort used the phrase 'mopping up'. After Ironside and Pownall had persuaded the French to launch a simultaneous attack with two divisions towards Cambrai, Gort's Command Post began to consider Franklyn's limited operation or sortie as part of the projected counter-attack to close the gap, yet, according to the Official History, no fresh orders were issued and Franklyn went ahead in happy ignorance of the French role.[26] This must have caused some puzzlement when Franklyn met Generals Prioux, Blanchard (1 Army), René Altmayer (V Corps), and Billotte, since Franklyn said he could not co-operate by attacking towards Bapaume. In the event the French were obliged to postpone their attack towards Cambrai because Altmayer's V Corps was too tired and disorganized by previous heavy fighting;[27] but the remnants of Prioux's 3 Light Armoured Division gallantly co-operated by protecting Franklyn's right flank.[28]

This is not the place for a description of the action at Arras except to say that Frankforce enjoyed an initial success out of all proportion to its size and even caused General Rommel (commanding 7 Panzer Division) to exaggerate

[25] *Keyes Diary* entries for 19, 20 and 21 May. The Diary includes the complete texts of the telegrams exchanged with the Prime Minister.

[26] Ellis pp. 87-91.

[27] The French liaison officer between 1st Army and Gort's GHQ, Commandant Vautrin, found General Altmayer tired out, thoroughly disheartened and weeping silently. 'He told me that one should see things as they are, that the troops had buggered off, that he was ready to accept all the consequences of his refusal (to attack on 21 May) and go and get himself killed at the head of a battalion, but he would no longer continue to sacrifice the army corps of which he had already lost nearly half'. Cited by Chapman p. 186. For the text of Vautrin's two reports, covering the periods December 1939-April 1940, and 18-26 May, 1940, see P. Reynaud *Au Coeur de la Mêlée* (Paris: Flammarion, 1951), pp. 551-63.

[28] On 20 May Archdale found there was no need to try to 'put heart into' General Prioux who, although he had only about thirty-five heavy Somua tanks left in his two light mechanized divisions (DLMs), was eager for the battle. For the British part in the Arras action see Brian Bond 'Arras, 21 May 1940. A Case Study in Counter-Stroke' in C. Barnett et al *Old Battles and New Defences* (Brassey's Defence Publishers, 1986) pp. 61-84.

the Allies' potential ability to counter-attack. What does call for comment is the poor intelligence work at GHQ, which committed a tiny improvised force (two territorial battalions and seventy-four tanks plus artillery and a motorcycle battalion without air cover) against enormously superior forces. These comprised chiefly two armoured divisions (5 and 7) and part of the SS Totenkopf Division. GHQ's failure to give Franklyn any orders after 20 May lends support to Guy Chapman's speculation that Gort reluctantly allowed himself to be pushed by Ironside and Churchill into an operation in which he did not believe.[29] Since neither the British nor French were ever fully informed as to what the other intended, both had genuine grounds for believing the other had let them down. The French were to be especially upset by Frankforce's withdrawal from Arras on the night of 23-24 May, although by then the small British force was nearly encircled.

Weygand's attempt on 21 May to co-ordinate plans for a counter-attack epitomized the difficulties that had bedevilled Allied strategy ever since 10 May. His message to Gort, mentioning a time and meeting place, like so many of Weygand's messages, was never received. In any case he encountered numerous snags on his journey and was forced to change the venue. He eventually arranged to meet the King of the Belgians and Billotte at Ypres on the afternoon of 21 May, but took no direct steps to inform Gort, who waited all day at his command post.

There were in fact three meetings at the Ypres Conference.[30] At the first Weygand met the King and Van Overstraeten; at the second they were joined by Generals Billotte and Fagalde (commanding XVI Corps); Weygand then left (for a hazardous return to Paris via England) before the third meeting at which Gort and Pownall joined the French and Belgians, who had waited for their arrival. Weygand's responsibilities in Paris were undeniably pressing but one must suspect an element of pique in his unwillingness to await the arrival of the British C-in-C.

The essential point of Weygand's plan was to concert an attack from north and south to pinch out the German corridor along the Somme, which was correctly thought to be precarious. The immediate problem was which divisions from 1 Army Group could take part from the north and how soon. At the first meeting (with the Belgians only) Weygand explained that the Belgian role would be to fall back to the Yser so as to shorten the line and safeguard the Allies' left flank and rear. Van Overstraeten replied that the Belgian Army could retreat no further without disintegrating. When Billotte arrived he declared wearily that the French 1 Army was tired and barely capable of defending itself; in his view only the BEF retained an offensive capacity. Weygand then proposed as a compromise that the Belgian Army

[29] Chapman pp. 186-7.
[30] *Pownall Diaries* pp. 329-32. *Overstraeten* pp. 647-59. *Keyes Diary* entries for 21 and 22 May. Ellis pp. 106-11. Chapman pp. 195-7. Reynaud *In the Thick of the Fight* (Cassell, 1955), pp. 350-7. Shirer (pp. 820-2) shows a marked lack of understanding of King Leopold's predicament.

should extend its present front and so free part of the BEF for offensive action. This clearly required Gort's assent but by the time he had been located at Premesques and brought to Ypres Weygand had left. Gort explained that the sortie at Arras was in progress at that moment; he had no reserves available for a counter-atack and could not remain on the Escaut. It was then agreed that the Belgian Army would withdraw to the Lys and the BEF to its original defences on the French frontier between Maulde and Halluin. The Belgians would relieve one British division on the left flank and French 1 Army would relieve two on the right. This would take a considerable time and it was agreed that the counter-attack could not begin before the 26th. It was evident to Gort and the French generals that sooner or later the Belgian Army would have to swing back to the Yser. King Leopold was extremely reluctant to contemplate this step not only because of the exhausted state of his troops and the enormous technical difficulties involved in a further withdrawal; but also for reasons of state, ie, it would mean abandoning all but a tiny segment of his country. However, Pownall particularly noted in his diary that the King did agree that if he were forced to withdraw from the Lys there would be no alternative to the Yser. Although the King's attitude is understandable, the resultant compromise was a very bad military solution. In contrast to the straight Yser line the Lys constituted a vulnerable re-entrant. If the hinge on the Lys at Menin-Halluin broke—and it was the obvious target—the Belgians would unavoidably be driven northward and a gap opened which the British would be unable to fill.

The British Official History rightly refers to the 'appalling absence of confidence' which the Ypres Conference revealed. King Leopold and Van Overstraeten had clearly already concluded that France was beaten, and the former had already made plain his hope that the British would realize this and retire northward, maintaining contact with his Army. For his part, Weygand felt unable to order the Belgians to withdraw to the Yser. Billotte was clearly a broken man with no confidence that the French could lead a counter-attack. As for the British, Gort was still willing to play his part loyally—through he stressed it could not be much more than a sortie—hence his enquiry to Keyes on leaving the meeting as to whether the Belgians regarded the British as 'awful dirty dogs'; but it can hardly be doubted that by this stage he and Pownall had little faith in either of their allies and were beginning to give priority to the survival of the BEF.[31]

---

[31] On balance the evidence supports the view that at the time of the Ypres Conference Gort and Pownall were still prepared to contemplate a southward move, or at least a sortie, provided the French gave a lead. For a favourable French interpretation of Gort's attitude see Lyet, *op. cit.* pp. 82-6. There can be no dispute, however, that Gort already regarded the BEF's situation as desperate and was thinking about the problems of embarkation. On 20 May Slessor urged him to make for Calais and Boulogne if possible where the RAF could provide fighter cover, rather than Ostend and Nieuport which were out of range. Gort rightly doubted whether the BEF could get so far west. Slessor, incidentally, was filled with admiration at Gort's calm demeanour 'in the grimmest position of any British Commander in history'. Slessor *The Central Blue* pp. 288-9.

Thus, not surprisingly, the conference closed in a very depressed atmosphere with very little settled. As if the Allies' cup of tribulations was not
already overflowing, General Billotte was fatally injured in a car crash on the
way back to his headquarters. Although he had been a failure as co-ordinator
of 1 Army Group, he alone of the French generals knew Weygand's plans
at first hand and the detailed arrangements made with King Leopold and
Lord Gort. Weygand permitted an interregnum of three days before the even
less dynamic Blanchard was confirmed as Billotte's successor. To say the
least, the prospects of the Weygand plan seemed inauspicious in the circumstances prevailing on 21 May.

4

The Failure of the Weygand Plan and the Belgian Surrender
22-28 May 1940

Despite the brave gesture of the sortie around Arras on 21 May, the situation of the BEF was already critical. On the previous day the enemy's armoured spearheads had reached the Channel coast and captured Albert, Doullens, Amiens, Abbeville and Montreuil. The whole area between the rivers Scarpe and Somme was in enemy hands; the BEF's line of communications was severed and the two divisions (12 and 23 Divisions) sent to guard this open flank had practically ceased to exist.

For the central and southern sectors of the BEF the last day on the Escaut, 22 May, was comparatively quiet, but in the northern sector 44 Division was heavily attacked as Bock vainly attempted to break through towards Courtrai. That night the BEF fell back to its old positions on the French frontier between Maulde and Halluin, while the Belgians conformed by withdrawing to the Lys—their last fortified position. Meanwhile the Arras garrison still held out at the southern tip of First Group of Armies and from there a thinly-held defence followed the canal line to Gravelines and the sea. Boulogne and Calais were still in Allied hands but between them and the canal line there was virtually nothing to stop the leading German divisions as they swung north-east towards Dunkirk.

Although the eastern front remained intact and was not under severe pressure, the BEF's prospects nevertheless appeared grim. Cut off from their supply base and nearly surrounded by a numerically superior enemy, the chances of escape in any direction seemed poor. German air supremacy became daily more marked: the Belgian air force had practically ceased to exist while the Air Component of the BEF was now almost entirely operating from England. Lord Gort was forced to improvise by sending additional scratch forces to join Macforce in providing a flimsy protective screen for his open western flank—initially some forty-five miles along the canal line from Carvin to St Momelin with no fewer than forty-four crossings. Each battalion was attempting to cover about seven miles. The BEF had not yet been engaged in enough intensive fighting to be short of ammunition, but on 23 May the troops

75

were put on half rations. It was in these inauspicious circumstances that Lord Gort had to organize the British component of the counter-attack agreed upon at the Ypres Conference.

Meanwhile the very rapidity of the German armoured forces' advance, far outstripping their supporting infantry, had caused acute anxiety at Army Group A headquarters. Rommel had conveyed to von Rundstedt an exaggerated impression of the British counter-attack at Arras and the latter had nervously anticipated an all-out effort by the Allies to cut through his narrow corridor along the Somme. By 22 May these fears were abating with the southern flank on the Somme more securely held and the infantry divisions of three armies moving up. Von Rundstedt, however, was now beginning to think about a period of rest and regrouping before the next major phase of the campaign—the drive south across the Somme. This is the primary explanation for the otherwise incredible 'halt order', by which the armoured forces of Army Group A were checked on the line Gravelines-St Omer-Béthune from 24 May to the early hours of 27 May, and which afforded the BEF a vital breathing space in their retreat to Dunkirk.[1] The origins and repercussions of the halt order will be more fully examined in the next chapter.

On 22 May Churchill visited Reynaud and Weygand in Paris. The latter, despite his tiring return journey from Ypres, was 'brisk, buoyant and incisive'; not content with a southward retreat by 1 Army Group, he insisted on a south-eastern drive from around Cambrai and Arras towards St Quentin. The whole discussion was vitiated by over-optimism due to ignorance of the true situation. Least excusable was Weygand's assurance that a new French army under General Frère, eighteen to twenty divisions strong, was forming along the Somme and would drive forward through Amiens to Arras. Churchill relates that to avoid misunderstandings he dictated a *resumé* of the plan and showed it to Weygand, yet the telegram he dispatched to Gort bore little relation to the true state of affairs. The first two paragraphs stated:

1. That the Belgian Army should withdraw to the line of the Yser and stand there, the sluices being opened.
2. That the British Army and the French First Army should attack south-west towards Bapaume and Cambrai at the earliest moment, certainly tomorrow, with about eight divisions, and with the Belgian Cavalry Corps on the right of the British.

The Belgian Army, despite the agreement wrung from King Leopold at Ypres, was unable to retreat to the Yser; and there was little likelihood of its Cavalry Corps joining in the counter-attack. There was no hope of the British and French together raising eight divisions even by 26 May, so that 'certainly tomorrow' was just empty rhetoric. The telegram also referred to 'general directions' received from the War Office but this meant nothing to GHQ. Pownall gave vent to his exasperation at this 'cigar butt strategy' in his diary:

[1] Ellis, pp. 114-23.

Here are Winston's plans again. Can nobody prevent him trying to conduct operations himself as a super Commander-in-Chief? How does he think we are to collect eight divisions and attack as he suggests? Have we no front to hold (which if it cracked would let in the flood)? He can have no conception of our situation and condition. Where are the Belgian Cavalry Corps? How is an attack like this to be staged involving three nationalities at an hour's notice? The man's mad.[2]

It is hard to avoid the conclusion that Weygand had misled the Prime Minister, though Churchill's determination to see a silver lining in the darkest cloud may also have contributed to the confusion. According to the French minutes of the meeting Weygand was far less definite about the role of the French army south of the Somme, stating merely that General Frère's forces would strike northward to 'increase the pressure on the enemy armour in the region of Amiens, Abbeville and Arras'. This impression is borne out by Weygand's first General Order issued later that day, in which he gave Frère's force the task of recapturing the Somme crossings. Even more remarkable, whereas Churchill imagined Frère's Army to be a formidable force of eighteen or twenty divisions, it comprised in reality only six divisions, three of them incomplete and strung out on a front of sixty-five miles. Weygand's modest expectation regarding the French forces south of the Somme was further underlined in a subsequent conversation with his son. He remarked:

I was too well aware of the weakness of the numbers at my disposal for the manning of the Aisne-Somme line to allow myself to indulge in any illusions regarding the strength of this thrust from the south—that is from the neighbourhood of Amiens. But I calculated that however feeble it might be, it would at least create an additional threat to the German flank, and thus increase the chances of success for the northern offensive.

He added that Frère's VII Army took so long to assemble that when it did eventually attack the Germans were firmly established and it hardly progressed at all beyond its prepared positions.

For the historian the most depressing aspect of this *contretemps* is the gulf between Weygand's hollow rhetoric and the actual situation. His Operation Order No 1 (Official History, pp. 112-13) is rightly described by Major Ellis as 'so indefinite as to be puzzling'. The German attack was to be prevented from 'making its way to the sea', yet the leading divisions had reached the sea two days earlier! In which sector were the Allied forces 'much too thick on the ground', and how was the BEF—already hard put to maintain its lines intact—to be moved in its entirety to the right? How could Weygand assume that an Anglo-French southward counter-attack would be protected on the east by the Belgian forces retiring in successive bounds to the line of the Yser; or that 'these counter-attacks will be supported by the entire strength of the British air forces based in Great Britain'? What was needed rather were

[2] Churchill pp. 57-9. *Pownall Diaries* p. 333.

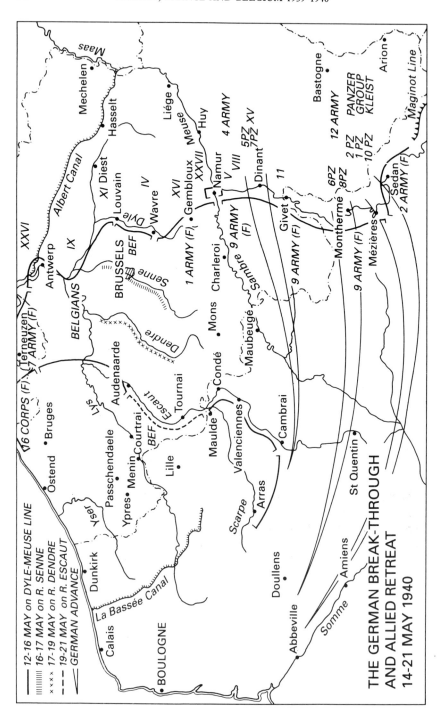

THE GERMAN BREAK-THROUGH
AND ALLIED RETREAT
14-21 MAY 1940

precise orders based on accurate intelligence of the enemy's strength and whereabouts to enable the commander of the First Group of Armies (and Blanchard was not confirmed in that appointment until 25 May) to co-ordinate his movements with those of the French forces advancing from south of the Somme. These conditions were never to be fulfilled in successive orders from Weygand and Georges which continued to ignore the crucial point made by Billotte at Ypres; namely that the First Group of Armies was so closely besieged that at best it could only mount sorties—the main effort to close the gap must be made from south of the Somme. This depressing fact was underlined by the French counter-attack east of Cambrai on 22 May, which Blanchard had been unable to stage the previous day in conjunction with the British operation at Arras. Instead of V Corps supported by two light armoured divisions, the size of the force was whittled down to one infantry regiment supported by two small armoured assault groups. Like Frankforce, the French group did well considering its size, but after reaching the outskirts of Cambrai that evening it was ordered to withdraw to avoid encirclement. This did not augur well for the major counter-offensive planned for 26 May.[3]

The interregnum in the direction of 1 Army Group following Billotte's fatal accident on 21 May only made confusion worse confounded. As Guy Chapman noted, the period between the evening of 23 May and the night of 25-26 May 'is one of the utmost confusion of crossed lines, misinformation and absence of information, of contradiction, of leaping to conclusions without verification, followed by suspicion, distrust and accusation.' Since the loss of Abbeville neither Weygand nor Georges could speak directly to 1 Army Group but could only relay messages via Belgian headquarters and London. Blanchard was reluctant to issue orders to the BEF and the Belgians until formally appointed, and in any case he was a military professor rather than a man of action who was already 'punch drunk' from the influx of depressing news. General Alan Brooke, who saw him at GHQ at Premesques on 24 May, felt that 'if he were to take over the tiller, it would not be long before we were on the rocks'. Two days later Marc Bloch was distressed to overhear Blanchard talking openly of capitulation.[4]

In view of the rather arrogant French assumption of superior wisdom in military matters vis-à-vis the British, which had been very noticeable during the period of Gamelin's command, it is interesting that in the crisis facing 1 Army Group several French generals implored Lord Gort to take command. On the morning of 24 May Guy Westmacott (British liaison officer with French III Corps) arrived at GHQ with a message from its dynamic commander, General Fornel de la Laurencie, begging Gort to take command of the French I Army. Major Archdale received a similar plea when he visited Lille. To

[3] Ellis pp. 111-13, 127-8. Shirer pp. 827-9. J. Weygand *The Role of General Weygand: Conversations with his Son* (Eyre & Spottiswoode, 1948. Henceforth referred to as 'J. Weygand'), p. 65.
[4] Chapman, pp. 203-5. Bloch p. 110.

all such overtures Gort replied that he could not interfere in the internal affairs of the French Army. Archdale noted several visits to GHQ by Blanchard, de la Laurencie, Prioux and Humbert who all realized that 'at Premesques alone was there still the capacity to command and the determination to take offensive action, if possible'. Even more remarkable, when Major General Sir Edward Spears (Churchill's liaison officer with Reynaud) took Archdale to see Pétain, the aged marshal made the startling suggestion: would General Gort assume command of all the Northern Armies? Spears rebuts the cynical inference that Pétain was trying to shift the burden of defeat to Britain's shoulders, and reflects that the British Government would never have placed the C-in-C in the impossible position of asking him to retrieve at the last moment an irretrievable situation. This is surely correct, yet at a War Cabinet meeting on 24 May Churchill wondered whether to approach Weygand with the suggestion that Dill be appointed to co-ordinate 1 Army Group. Ironside dissuaded him on the grounds that Georges had confidence in Blanchard and that the French would not fight so well under a British general.[5]

Few episodes during the retreat did more to sour Anglo-French relations than Gort's withdrawal of the Arras garrison (5 and 50 Divisions) on the night of 23-24 May. By that evening the town was closely invested on three sides, while to the north the enemy's pincers were only a few miles apart. Gort decided nothing was to be gained by sacrificing the garrison and countermanded his order to hold the town 'to the last man and the last round'. From the British viewpoint the successful withdrawal during the night some twenty-five kilometres north to the Canal Line was justifiable, but Blanchard was not immediately and fully informed of Gort's intentions—though a liaison officer was sent to the Command Post of the French 1 Light Mechanized Division (DLM)—and the fact remains that French I Army was left deployed in an uncomfortably narrow pocket between Maulde, Condé, Valençiennes and Douai. That night Blanchard sent a telegram to Weygand placing a hostile interpretation on Gort's order. Weygand then informed Reynaud, who at once indignantly telegraphed Churchill. Gort's action had been much magnified and distorted in transmission so that, according to Reynaud's message:

> The British Army had carried out a withdrawal forty kilometres in the direction of the ports at a moment when French forces from the south were gaining ground towards the Allied Armies of the North. The British withdrawal had obliged General Weygand to modify his whole plan. He was now compelled to give up his attempt to close the breach and establish a continuous front.

Churchill at once replied, rebutting the more sweeping accusations, but he was handicapped and exasperated by lack of information from Gort. In fact the BEF had not withdrawn forty kilometres in the direction of the ports; only two divisions had been withdrawn twenty-five kilometres to the Canal

[5] *Archdale Diary* entries dated 23, 24 and 26 May. Sir Edward Spears *Assignment to Catatrophe* (Heinemann, 1954), p. 228. References are to the one volume Reprint Society edition (1956). Colville pp. 213-14. Cab 65/7 137(40), 24 May.

Line. In any case Gort had not been ordered to hold the Arras salient, which was indeed outside the British sector, nor had he abandoned the projected counter-attack. Weygand's insinuation that the British had disrupted his plan by withdrawing at the very moment when the forces south of the Somme were stretching out to meet them was simply untrue.

While the tactical British withdrawal from Arras did not improve the prospects for the coming counter-attack, it was certainly used by some of the French generals as an alibi. Thus General Besson, commanding VI and VII Armies south of the Somme, rang General Frère on the evening of 24 May to say that owing to 1 Army Group's withdrawal his offensive could no longer be envisaged for the present. Their forces must form a line on the Somme and establish themselves in depth. Weygand advised Blanchard that if the British withdrawal had rendered the counter-attack impractical he should set up as wide a bridgehead as possible covering Boulogne, Calais and Dunkirk. This must have perplexed Blanchard because only the previous evening Weygand had given him an exaggerated report on the progress of the French VII Army suggesting it had already crossed the Somme. Commandant Pierre Lyet neatly summed up the pessimism of the French high command on 24 May as follows: 'While General Blanchard sent a liaison officer to Paris to explain the *difficulties* of the projected manoeuvre, General Weygand realized it was *impossible* and General Besson ordered its *abandonment*' (Lyet's italics).[6]

Despite Weygand's accusations, hastily underwritten by Reynaud, Gort and Blanchard had not in fact abandoned their part in the counter-attack to begin on 26 May, although neither was particularly sanguine. Early on 24 May Pownall wrote in his diary concerning the withdrawal from Arras just completed:

> This will not take away from the possibility of attack southwards in conjunction with First Army, as projected yesterday, since the withdrawal of 5th and 50th enables these divisions to be used for the purpose.

That same afternoon Generals Sir Ronald Adam (III Corps) and René Altmayer (French V Corps) discussed the operation with Blanchard at his headquarters at Attiche. The idea was to drive south on both sides of the Canal du Nord towards Bapaume and Péronne. The French would provide three divisions and the British two (5 and 50 Divisions). French and British cavalry would protect the open Douai flank and the RAF would provide bomber and fighter air cover. Those forces would concentrate on the 25th; occupy bridgeheads over the Sensée on the 26th; and advance south on either side of the Canal du Nord on the morning of the 27th.[7]

[6] Lyet pp. 93-8. Ellis pp. 132, 141-3. Shirer pp. 830-3.
[7] *Pownall Diaries* pp. 336-7. Chapman p. 206. It is perhaps some indication of the vagueness of 1st Army Group's intended counter-attack of 26 May that its objective is variously given as Bapaume, St Quentin, Péronne and Cambrai.

Before explaining the circumstances in which Gort personally decided to cancel the British part in this operation, it is necessary to describe the wave of defeatism which was now beginning to engulf the French high command and government.

General Spears, Churchill's personal liaison officer with the French Government, arrived in Paris on 25 May. Spears, although a Francophile, was highly sensitive to the French tendency to blame her allies for any failure, and he at once determined not to let any anti-British remark pass unchallenged.[8] The possibility of a French surrender was brought home to him on the very day of his arrival when Blanchard's emissary, Major Fauvelle, explained the position north of the Somme. Present were Reynaud, Pétain, Weygand, Darlan, Baudouin and Spears. Fauvelle, according to Spears's rather partisan account, was the very embodiment of catastrophe: 'I have in my time seen broken men, but never before one deliquescent, that is in a state when he was fit only to be scraped up with a spoon or mopped up'. When Reynaud asked him about the condition of Blanchard's Army he made the astonishing reply 'I believe in a very early capitulation'. The Prime Minister roundly condemned such defeatism, but Weygand then indulged in a long tirade 'in a voice like a saw on steel', the burden of which was 'This war is sheer madness, we have gone to war with a 1918 army against a German army of 1939'. Infected by Fauvelle's despondency, Weygand began to argue that the only course open to the Northern Armies was to fall back to the harbours. Reynaud and Spears both challenged him on the grounds that Blanchard's counter-attack was about to begin and might yet succeed. In contrast to his earlier optimism Weygand now showed that he had no confidence in a break-through southward. Spears recalls that at that moment he suddenly realized what he had only dimly sensed before: that for the French the sea was much the same thing as an abyss of boiling pitch and brimstone. Withdrawal to Dunkirk for them consequently meant retiring into a fortress from which there could be no escape. Spears's attempt to argue that evacuation would be but a prelude to continuing the fight elsewhere was received in glum silence. As a result of this painful meeting Spears's confidence in Weygand declined sharply,[9] but his admiration and sympathy for Reynaud, surrounded by defeatists, increased.

At a War Committee meeting that same evening (25 May) the possibility of France withdrawing from the war was openly discussed, though which

[8] Spears was a splendid embodiment of Churchillian pugnacity, but whether his robust style of diplomacy always had the desired effect on the French may be doubted. For example, when Fauvelle asked whether Britain would bomb France if the latter made peace, Spears replied: 'Certainly, just as you have bombed Belgian and Dutch towns that have been unable to defend themselves, we shall attack and bomb every place that harbours a German, regardless of who else may be there'. Spears p. 198.

[9] *Ibid* p. 200, 'The more I thought of Weygand ... the less confident did I become. He was gradually to assume in my thoughts the aspect of a jack-in-the-box, a very ancient toy whose vivacity still startled, though he had but one trick to play'.

minister first mentioned the word 'armistice' was to be bitterly disputed for years. Certainly by the end of the long and acrimonious meeting Pétain, Weygand, President Lebrun and Reynaud had all posed the 'possibility of ceasing hostilities and enquiring what terms the enemy would offer'. Reynaud agreed to fly to London the following day to discover the British Government's reaction to the possibility of France making a separate peace. On his return, however, Reynaud curtly told Baudouin: 'I did not raise the question'. Eden recollects that the French Prime Minister brought disturbing accounts of Marshal Pétain's defeatism. Churchill records that 'M. Reynaud dwelt not obscurely upon the possible French withdrawal from the war'.[10] Thus even before the British evacuation from Dunkirk began some of the most powerful members of the French Government regarded the war as lost.

As was seen in the previous chapter Sir Roger Keyes, from his vantage point with the King of the Belgians, was quick to appreciate the precarious situation of the BEF. Convinced that an attempt to counter-attack to the south would result in disaster he repeatedly attempted to persuade the British Government to permit a retreat to the Channel ports. On 22 May, for example, both Keyes and Gort's ADC, Lord Munster, telephoned to the Secretary of State for War (Anthony Eden) from La Panne. Keyes suggested that General Dill (VCIGS) be sent out to GHQ to see how bad things were for himself. At 10.30 am on 24 May Keyes spoke to Churchill who, having just been falsely reassured by Weygand that the attack from south of the Somme was making good progress, insisted that the BEF would march south. In despair Keyes begged Churchill to send out Dill and the latter came over to Ostend that night in a motor torpedo boat.

Dill reached GHQ early on the morning of 25 May. He brought no cheering news and even hinted that there was criticism at home that the BEF 'with 200,000 men who claimed to be better fighters than the Boche', were not doing enough. General Blanchard and his chief of staff arrived during Dill's visit and the former confirmed that he would participate in the counter-attack with two or three divisions supported by 200 tanks. Although Blanchard made it clear that the main effort would have to come from south of the Somme he had evidently not abandoned the operation as a result of the British withdrawal from Arras. Nor apparently had he been informed that, according to Reynaud's telegram to London, Weygand had been compelled to give up his attempt to close the breach the previous day.

Consequently, although Dill in his report to the Prime Minister stressed the difficulties of the BEF's situation, he also confirmed that the operation would be carried out as planned. At 1.00 pm, Keyes escorted Dill to an interview with King Leopold and Van Overstraeten. All three were dismayed

---

[10] *Ibid* pp. 180-2, 187-8, 190-7, 214. Baudouin pp. 45-56. Shirer pp. 837-40. Churchill pp. 61-3, 108. The Earl of Avon *The Eden Memoirs: The Reckoning* (Cassell, 1965—henceforth referred to as 'Eden'), p. 111.

at his optimism in insisting that the counter-attack must go ahead despite the critical situation on the Belgian front. Between 3.00 and 5.00 pm Major Archdale was at GHQ arranging liaison duties for the following day. As he recalled, Gort was sitting at his table, very silent, and looking rather bewildered and bitter. He complained that he had had a raw deal from the French; not only had their Army continually pleaded that it was too tired to fight, and their staff work broken down, but from start to finish there had been no direction or information from the High Command. Why, he asked, did they retreat to the Escaut when they knew of the great gap in the middle: why not retreat south and preserve a front and lines of communications?

At 5.00 pm Gort was still determined to implement the counter-attack whatever the difficulties, but about an hour later he took what the official historian describes as 'perhaps his most fateful action during the whole campaign'. Without consulting the British Government or asking authority from the French commander, he ordered 5 and 50 Divisions to abandon preparations for the attack southwards and to move at once to plug the threatening gap between the British and Belgian armies between Menin and Ypres, thus preserving the escape route to Dunkirk.[11]

There was bitter irony in the fact that the one crucial decision which Gort, the fighting general *par excellence*, had to make during the entire campaign was to call off the counter-attack. He was doubtless influenced by a telephone call from General Adam that Altmayer could after all only provide one division for the attack; but the major consideration was the news that the Belgian Army was disintegrating under a fierce onslaught. Bock had thrown four divisions against the Belgian-held Courtrai sector of the Lys on the previous afternoon (24 May) and by nightfall the enemy was across the river between Wijk and Courtrai to a depth of one and a half miles on a thirteen-mile front. Colonel Lumsden (12th Lancers) reported—unjustly—that the Belgians were showing no fighting spirit, and on leaving GHQ at 7.30 pm on 25 May Archdale found Ypres and the surrounding area strangely quiet and deserted. The line in front of Ypres seemed almost non-existent, and there was no sign of support troops in the rear. In fact the Belgian Army had made a valiant effort to seal the breach but was driven inexorably northward by an enemy superior in numbers and in total command of the air. Gort at once informed General Altmayer that the attack was off, but—as in the withdrawal from Arras—was unable to contact Blanchard in person to explain his sudden move.[12]

Gort's decision to abandon the counter-attack and concentrate on saving as much as possible of the BEF is easy to support, particularly from a British viewpoint. There was abundant evidence that under Blanchard's ineffectual

---

[11] *Keyes Diary* entries for 22-25 May. *Pownall Diaries* pp. 339-40. Ellis pp. 147-8. *Archdale Diary* entry for 25 May. Overstraeten p. 685.
[12] Ellis pp. 135-6, 146-9. Shirer p. 842. *Pownall Diaries* pp. 338-40. Colville pp. 216-17.

leadership French I Army would not be able to make a significant contribution to the operation. More seriously, GHQ had rightly become sceptical of exaggerated reports of the progress made by French forces advancing from south of the Somme alternating with rumours that these operations had been abandoned. There never was in reality a co-ordinated 'Weygand Plan'; instead the French commanders north and south of the Somme each expected the other's forces to play the major role, while Weygand himself was never able to exert effective control of his own forces. Consequently he issued a series of 'stop-go' reports and orders which only further confused not only his own generals but also the British Government and Gort's headquarters. On 24 May, for example, Gort was informed from London that 'Weygand reports French VII Army is advancing successfully and has captured Albert, Péronne and Amiens'. Had this been true it would have meant that the French had not only swept aside the strong German garrisons on the Somme crossings, but had advanced well to the north of the river to Albert—about a quarter of the distance separating them from the northern armies. In that case Gort would have faced a serious charge of ruining the only measure which might have thwarted a German victory. Subsequent information justified his scepticism. General Besson's forces, so far from recapturing Albert, never succeeded in even taking the Somme bridgeheads.[13]

The Weygand Plan had in fact already been dead for several days before— in French eyes—Gort 'killed' it by his independent decision. Perhaps if any criticism can be levelled at Gort on this score it is that he was doggedly loyal to the ineffectual Blanchard and the French High Command for too long. He might have decided even earlier to make for the Channel ports as Weygand and Reynaud alleged that he had. By delaying this unpleasant decision to the last possible moment he risked the encirclement of the BEF. Thanks to Allied valour in defence—but also to the wrangles and contradictory orders of the German High Command—the great majority of British troops were successfully evacuated. What is less often emphasized is that by persisting in attempts to implement the Weygand Plan Britain and France were instrumental in precipitating Belgium's collapse through over-extension to assist the BEF.

An issue which must be raised, though the answer can only be tentative, is whether the BEF could have done more to relieve the Belgians by counterattacking Bock's left flank as the Germans attacked *across* the BEF's well fortified front towards Courtrai. Between 24 and 26 May the Belgian High Command made at least five appeals by messenger and signal to the effect that the only hope of averting a disaster was for the British to strike at the vulnerable German flank between the Escaut and the Lys. Keyes, for example, transmitted the following message to GHQ:

[13] Chapman pp. 198-9, 203. Shirer pp. 831-3, 843.

Van Overstraeten is desperately keen for strong British counter-attack. Either north or south of Lys could help restore situation. Belgians expect to be attacked on Ghent front tomorrow. Germans already have bridgehead over canal west of Eecloo. There can be no question of Belgian withdrawal to Yser. One battalion on march NE of Ypres was practically wiped out today in attack by sixty aircraft. Withdrawal over open roads without adequate fighter support very costly. Whole of their supplies are east of Yser. They strongly represent attempt should be made to restore situation on Lys by British counter-attack for which opportunity may last another few hours only. Sending officer to explain that view.

The BEF in its well-prepared defences between Halluin and Bourghelles was in a good position to relieve the pressure on the Belgian Army, which was not only outnumbered on the ground but the victim of tremendous low-level bombing attacks without respite. The Belgians correctly pointed out that the British divisions on the enemy's flank had not suffered any such ordeal by bombing nor had they been seriously engaged in recent days. This is borne out by the British Official History. Of 26 May, the third quiet day in succession for the BEF on the eastern front, Major Ellis writes:

> British divisions in the old Frontier Line were not seriously attacked though they were subjected to heavy shelling. From our forward positions considerable bodies of enemy troops were seen in the distance moving northwards across our front, but by now it was essential to husband carefully the very meagre supplies of ammunition which remained and the artillery were forced to let them pass unmolested. Yet the position on our left grew hourly more threatening as Belgian withdrawals under heavy attack widened the gap between our left and their right.

Van Overstraeten lamented that the magnificent troops of the BEF were being wasted in futile marches and counter-marches. He appreciated that it might be difficult for Lord Gort to mount his artillery for such an attack because of the preparations to implement the Weygand Plan, but he pointed out that the German divisions crossing the British front were largely composed of infantry. A local success here would not only encourage the Belgians but would also ensure the retention of two more ports for evacuation, namely Ostend and Nieuport.

Gort and Brooke (II Corps) turned deaf ears to these appeals. Certainly their position was extremely difficult with an undefended gap opening up on their flank around Ypres. The British official historian concludes that 'a counter-attack here (between the Lys and Escaut) was out of the question, for the only British units not already engaged were being hurried northward to close the gap'. Brooke, he adds, had neither troops nor ammunition for counter-attack elsewhere. Sir Basil Liddell Hart challenged this verdict, in the present author's view persuasively. He stressed the comparatively quiet time enjoyed by the British divisions on the frontier during the previous three days and queried why at least parts of 5 and 50 Divisions (released from the southward move) could not have counter-attacked as the Belgians wished. He also computed, from the figures supplied by the Official History, that after the first phase of plugging the Ypres gap the odds against General Franklyn, commanding a considerably reinforced 5 Division, were only 9:7. This comment is not meant as a criticism either of the courage or the skilful manoeuvring by which Brooke and his subordinates frustrated the German attempt to infiltrate the gap left by the retreating Belgians. Rather it is suggested that a counter-attack to relieve pressure on the Belgians was feasible had Gort and his subordinates been minded to try.

Why they did not can be explained by enumerating the BEF's own problems, but there is evidence to suggest that by now the British commanders were confirmed in their anti-Belgian prejudices and would be unwilling to take risks to assist them. As Pownall wrote in his diary early on 26 May, referring to a retreat to the Channel coast: 'We need not fear Germans following us up. What we have to fear is a Belgian break which would let the enemy across the Ypres Canal. The Belgians show every sign of running fast northwards... We have sent every message we can think of to try and get them to stand where we want them (sic). But they are rotten to the core and in the end we shall have to look after ourselves'. Weygand also criticized Gort for not counter-attacking more vigorously on the Lys though Spears seems to have misinterpreted his remark.[14]

Blanchard was probably relieved that Gort had taken the initiative in calling off preparations for the counter-attack. At 11.30 pm on 25 May he issued a general order stating that in view of the German breakthrough on the Lys and the withdrawal of the two British divisions to meet this emergency the operations planned for the following day were cancelled. Instead the three Allied armies were ordered to regroup behind the water-line demarcated by the Aa Canal, the Lys and the Canal de Dérivation for the purpose of forming a bridgehead covering Dunkirk in depth. There was no suggestion that this withdrawal northward was a prelude to embarkation. Weygand received Blanchard's order on the morning of 26 May, approved it and authorized the withdrawal. Yet although the 'Weygand Plan' was now definitely dead this did not prevent its author from again wiring Blanchard with the false information that General Frère's VII Army was about to cross the Somme. So the myth was revived that Gort's withdrawal had caused the failure of the counter-attack. Weygand, and to a lesser extent Reynaud, were confirmed in their prejudice that in an emergency a British commander would always make for the harbours.[15]

Gort and Pownall visited Blanchard's headquarters on the morning of 26 May and drew up lines of retirement beginning that night with the BEF pulling back to the Béthune-Armentières Canal. Pownall emphasized that they did not discuss any question of going to the sea 'though I have a strong suspicion that was really in the minds of the French, as it certainly was

[14] Ellis pp. 146, 176-7, 194, 196 (Liddell Hart's copy with his marginal comments). *Overstraeten* pp. 689-90, 695-8, 707, 710, 725. *Keyes Diary* entry for 26 May. *Pownall Diaries* pp. 342-5. Baudouin p. 59. Spears p. 247.
[15] Baudouin pp. 56-60. Spears pp. 180, 182. Lyet pp. 102-3. Shirer pp. 842-4.

in ours'. On their return to GHQ they found a message from Eden advising Gort that 'safety of BEF will be predominant consideration. In such conditions the only course open to you may be to fight your way back to coast where all beaches and ports east of Gravelines will be used for embarkation'. This was pretty definite despite the conditional 'may', and a second telegram from Eden was even more specific. It stated that Churchill had informed Reynaud in London that day of the British intention and the latter had agreed to ask Weygand to issue the necessary instructions. 'You are now authorized', Eden concluded, 'to operate towards the coast forthwith in conjunction with the French and Belgian Armies'.

It is scarcely credible that in this dire emergency the three allies should have left even the slightest room for misunderstanding of their intentions, but in fact the muddle and mutual recrimination which had characterized the whole campaign continued until the very end. Gort may perhaps be excused for not informing the Belgians immediately on 26 May that the BEF intended to embark, since he regarded it as a political decision, but there is no defence for the Government's silence. The confusion on the French side is harder to understand. Weygand had approved Blanchard's order to withdraw to a bridgehead covering Dunkirk: furthermore he knew of the British Admiralty's preparations for possible evacuation and on 26 May telephoned Admiral Darlan to discuss the possibility of evacuating all the forces in Flanders from Dunkirk. Darlan was reluctant to contemplate this operation. Yet Weygand failed to inform either Blanchard or Admiral Abrial, in charge of the Dunkirk area, that French as well as British troops might well have to be embarked. The explanation seems to be that Weygand clung to the remarkable view that the bridgehead could hold 'for an indefinite length of time' until it could be used as a springboard for a counter-offensive. But as generalissimo should he not have made sure that the British Government accepted this plan? Thus Blanchard, contrary to what Gort and Pownall assumed, believed that his mission was to stand on the Lys to the bitter end. Indeed, until 29 May that actually was his mission. If Weygand had intended to embitter Anglo-French relations at the height of the military crisis he could hardly have done so more effectively.[16]

By midnight on 26 May, when 'Operation Dynamo' officially began, the Royal Navy had already evacuated nearly 28,000 non-fighting troops. By then, however, Boulogne was in German hands and Calais was about to fall; it also seemed unlikely that Ostend would be available. Only Dunkirk and the eastward beaches remained and enemy bombing threatened to render the harbour impracticable. On 27 May the Germans advanced to within four miles of Dunkirk, so bringing the port and its approaches within artillery

[16] Eden pp. 110-11. *Pownall Diaries* pp. 342-4. J. Weygand pp. 71-5. John C. Cairns 'Great Britain and the Fall of France' in *Journal of Modern History*, December 1955, p. 373.

range. It is easy to understand the pessimistic estimates that only a small fraction of the BEF would escape.

At 7.00 am on 27 May, just as the Germans began attacking the town, a conference was held at Cassel to organize the Dunkirk bridgehead. Sir Ronald Adam had been delegated to command the British sector and Fagalde the French, both under the direction of Admiral Abrial. Also present were Blanchard, Prioux and Weygand's representative, General Koeltz. Koeltz read out a stirring message from Weygand proposing a march to relieve Calais, which had by then capitulated. None of the Frenchmen present had any thought of evacuation. When Gort eventually caught up with Koeltz that evening he enquired 'Since you come from General Weygand, what do you know about the plan for embarking 30,000 men a day?' Koeltz answered: 'I've never heard it mentioned'. This augured ill for French I Army, most of which was still south of the Lys.[17]

On the morning of 28 May the bulk of Prioux's I Army was still in the Lille area and was in danger of being cut off. Unless the French moved promptly they would be isolated when the BEF retired that night from the Lys to the line Cassel-Poperinghe-Ypres (Gort now regarded evacuation as a matter of extreme urgency since the Belgian cease-fire had taken effect at 4.00 am on 28 May). Yet when Blanchard visited GHQ that morning he was horrified to learn of Gort's intention to leave the Lys that night with a view to evacuation. Gort and Pownall failed to get him to change his mind after a long, exasperating discussion. They appreciated that if the BEF withdrew independently and virtually the whole of French I Army was captured, they would be blamed for deserting their ally.

Blanchard later changed his mind but left it to Prioux to decide when and how much of I Army would withdraw. Prioux eventually decided that only his III Corps and what remained of the Cavalry Corps should withdraw, starting at midday on 29 May. When, however, Major General E. A. Osborne, commanding 44 Division on the right of the French, in the south-west corner of the pocket, called at III Corps headquarters at 9.00 pm, he was astonished to be told that General de la Laurencie proposed to start at 11.00 pm that night. Osborne, who was already angry with Prioux for not informing him that part of I Army would after all retreat when earlier in the day he had obstinately refused to move, was received 'with informal rudeness' by de la Laurencie. To all Osborne's questions about timing and routes he merely repeated 'onze heures'. Prioux himself remained to be taken prisoner with a large part of IV and V Corps on 29 May. The garrison of Lille, commanded by General Molinié, maintained a heroic defence until the evening of 31 May, when it surrendered with the honours of war—a rare distinction in the

---

[17] Chapman pp. 218-19. Colville p. 220. A Prioux *Souvenirs de guerre* (Paris: Flammarion, 1947), p. 122. Churchill in London was unable to keep abreast of events: on 27 May, for example, he exhorted Gort to occupy Ostend with a brigade of artillery and send a column to relieve Calais 'while it is still holding out'. Churchill p. 80.

Second World War. Only on the afternoon of 29 May, three days after the British evacuation had begun and over 70,000 troops had been embarked, did Weygand authorize the evacuation of as large a part as possible of I French Army. Despite the predominance of British shipping, Gort agreed under orders that henceforth an equal number of French troops would be embarked.[18]

Until the British attack on her Mediterranean fleet after France had sought an armistice, the event which caused most hatred and vilification among the Allies was surely the King of the Belgians' unilateral request for a ceasefire on the evening of 27 May. In the agonizing tension of those days it is possible to understand why some of the malicious calumnies were cast upon the unhappy King and his advisers. What is surprising is the resilience and longevity of accusations which were disputed at the time and subsequently shown to be baseless. King Leopold's policy is open to criticism but the time is long past when the Belgians can be conveniently treated as a scapegoat.[19]

Reichenau's VI Army launched a ferocious attack on the Belgian IV Corps on either side of Courtrai on the afternoon of 24 May. It was the beginning of the end. The Lys was crossed above and below the town: Belgian reserves were thrown in but failed to restore the situation. At nightfall the Belgians still held Menin but their Army was swinging back as the Germans drove towards Iseghem. On the morning of 25 May the Belgian High Command informed Gort that the situation was becoming critical. They were being attacked along their whole front and had no more reserves to extend their right to keep in touch with the British at Menin. As for a retreat to the Yser—on which the Allies were counting—they regretted that it was impossible because the manoeuvre (along roads crammed with refugees and devoid of air cover) would destroy their Army more rapidly than a battle and without loss to the enemy. The best they could do was to prepare an anti-tank barrier of railway trucks between Ypres and Roulers, and to open the sluices between Ypres and Nieuport. As we have seen, Gort responded by sending two divisions to plug the gap on his left and then to extend his line along the Yser towards Dixmude, but he felt unable to counter-attack to relieve German pressure on the Lys.[20]

---

[18] Ellis pp. 208-10, 219. *Pownall Diaries* pp. 347-50 (a typed copy of Osborne's report is enclosed in the original diary). Lyet pp. 110-11. Prioux pp. 117-36. Chapman pp. 220-3.

[19] Emile Cammaerts' *The Prisoner at Laeken: King Leopold Legend and Fact* (London: The Cresset Press, June 1941), though avowedly sympathetic to the King, examines all the accusations against him thoroughly and fairly. Cammaerts, a Belgian man of letters and an academic long resident in England, stresses that the disagreement between the King and his Ministers concerned genuine political issues; both had Belgium's interests at heart. He does not therefore attempt to justify the King's decision to remain in Belgium by castigating the Ministers for leaving. Curiously, Shirer, in *The Collapse of the Third French Republic*, omits Cammaerts's book from his bibliography and relies heavily on sources critical of Leopold. By far the most detailed and thoroughly researched account sympathetic to the King is Roger Keyes *Outrageous Fortune* (1984).

[20] O. Michiels *18 Jours de guerre en Belgique* (Paris: Berger-Levrault, 1947), p. 211. Chapman pp. 208-9. Keyes mistakenly informed the Cabinet that the Belgian Army would have fallen back to the Yser by 24 May (Cab 65/7 136(40), 23 May). Liddell Hart noted that on the map in Ellis, facing p. 182, showing the situation on the evening of 26 May the three German divisions

Whether the Belgians had just cause for resentment at the British failure to do anything positive to help them may be argued; the former had after all extended their right wing as far as Menin in order to free British divisions for the counter-attack. They were certainly justified in resenting their allies' failure to keep them fully informed of their intentions. Eden admits that he wrote to the Prime Minister on the night of 26 May to remind him that they had told the Belgians nothing about the change of plan (ie, to retreat to the Channel coast and embark), though they had authorized Gort to do so. Eden suggested that Churchill advise King George VI personally to send this news or do so himself. Eden feared lest the British withdrawal should crack Belgian resolve, already weakened by defeat.

There is some evidence that this happened. The Belgian Chief of Staff, General Michiels, records that troop movements behind the British lines and destruction of stores caused them to suspect on 25 May that the BEF was withdrawing, and by the next day the Belgians felt they had been left to their own devices. That afternoon (26 May) Michiels sent a message to Weygand, warning him that the situation of the Belgian Army was grave and that the C-in-C intended to carry on the fight until all means were exhausted. The enemy was even then attacking from Eecloo to Menin. The limits of resistance had nearly been reached. No reply was received. Was it realistic to expect the Belgians to fight to the last to enable the Allies to escape by sea? That that is precisely what Churchill did expect is evident from his message to Gort, dated 27 May. After urging Gort to send a column to relieve Calais he wrote:

> It is now necessary to tell the Belgians. I am sending following telegram to Keyes, but your personal contact with the King is desirable. Keyes will help. We are asking them to sacrifice themselves for us.

Although Churchill's enclosure for Keyes was not delivered to the Admiral before he returned to England on 28 May, it is worth quoting in full for the light it sheds on the Prime Minister's attitude to Belgium:

> Impart following to your friend (the King of the Belgians). Presume he knows that British and French are fighting their way to coast between Gravelines and Ostend inclusive, and that we propose to give fullest support from Navy and Air Force during hazardous embarkation. What can we do for him? Certainly we cannot serve Belgium's cause by being hemmed in and starved out. Our only hope is victory, and England will never quit the war whatever happens till Hitler is beat or we cease to be a State. Trust you will make sure he leaves with you by aeroplane before too late. Should our operation prosper and we establish an effective bridgehead, we would try, if desired, to carry some Belgian divisions to France by sea. Vitally important Belgium should continue in war, and safety of King's person essential.[21]

(18, 31 and 61 Divisions) shown against the line held by 5 Division between Ypres and the Lys were not yet attacking. In general Ellis does not stress sufficiently that between 24 and 27 May the enemy was passing *across* the BEF's front to attack the Belgians on the Lys.
[21] Michiels pp. 208-12. Eden p. 111. Churchill p. 80.

By this time Gort and Pownall were so prejudiced against the Belgians that they were always anticipating the worst and did not give credit where it was due. Certainly they had several legitimate grounds for complaint but there were instances where the Belgians were more sinned against than sinning. It is a pity that the GHQ view has often been uncritically accepted as the whole story through the authoritative impression conveyed by Gort's Dispatches and through Pownall's advisory role both to Churchill's *History of the Second World War* and the Official History. A very different version is contained in the unpublished memoirs of Lieutenant Colonel (later Brigadier) George Davy, head of the British Military Mission at Belgian headquarters. In theory Davy's mission was intended for liaison between the War Office and King Leopold's headquarters, but he at once discovered that liaison between Gort's HQ and the Belgians had broken down. Consequently on several occasions between 17 and 27 May, Davy personally intervened to improve liaison in the field between the British left and the Belgian right flanks. In his opinion poor British staff work was more often to blame for frequent loss of contact. As for the GHQ accusation that the Belgians were always pulling back without prior notification, Davy mentions three occasions when the Belgians held on after the BEF had withdrawn—most notably on the Escaut, where they relieved the exhausted British 44 Division and allowed it to retire through their ranks. Davy, whose loyalties were put to a severe test, also mentions remarks which reveal the feelings of contempt for the Belgians that were entertained at GHQ. On 23 May, for example, when he enquired of Gort and Pownall whether some of the Belgian troops might be evacuated with the BEF, he recalls Pownall replying 'We don't care a bugger what happens to the Belgians'. Gort made no dissenting comment. Pownall's consistently hostile attitude to the Belgians in his diary makes such a remark entirely credible, and Brooke held similar views. Keyes, though a less disinterested witness than Davy, also thought the British were over-critical towards the Belgians. When, on the evening of 26 May, Gort sent King Leopold what amounted to a reprimand for withdrawing northward and thereby exposing the British left flank, Keyes suppressed the message. Both during and after the campaign Keyes and Davy attempted to present the Belgian record in the best light, and more recently their efforts have been reinforced by the present Lord Keyes' detailed and generally persuasive biography *Outrageous Fortune*.[22]

During the final week of Belgium's resistance King Leopold rejected increasingly urgent pleas to flee the country not only from his own ministers but from the British Government. The King, fortified in his decision by the

[22] G. M. O. Davy *Unpublished Memoirs* chapter 13; Supplementary Report (5 pp.) sent to the Official Historian on 24 September 1943; Note (5 pp.) to Nyssens (former Belgian liaison officer at Gort's GHQ dated 8 September 1949(?). *Keyes Diary* 10-28 May 1940 *passim*. Reynaud in *In the Thick of the Fight* (an abridged translation of *Au Coeur de la Mêlée*, Cassell, 1955), pp. 420-41 adopts a more statesmanlike attitude towards the Belgian surrender than he displayed in 1940. David Divine is one British writer who takes a sympathetic view of the Belgian war effort, see *The Nine Days of Dunkirk* (Faber, 1959), pp. 236-41. Keyes *Outrageous Fortune* p. 179ff.

support of the Queen Mother, remained unshaken in the view that his duty was in the first place to remain with his Army as C-in-C, thus prolonging resistance as long as possible and, second, in the event of defeat and German occupation to share the ordeal of his people. His ministers pointed out that the latter aim, though laudable, was impracticable since the King would lose his authority and become merely a prisoner in a royal palace. Leopold informed his ministers that if they fled the country against his wishes, they would cease to constitute the legal government. When the British Government's offer of sanctuary was declined by the King, Churchill asked King George VI to reply in person to a letter from Leopold explaining his motives. The essential part of his telegram—representing the Government's rather than his own personal view—which Keyes received at 6.00 am on 27 May, was as follows:

> While it would be presumptuous of me to advise you in respect of your duty to your people, I can say that as regards the Allies and the fulfilment of their joint purpose in war, I do not feel that Your Majesty is called upon to make the sacrifice which you contemplate.
> Moreover, I am bound to put to Your Majesty another point. If it were possible for You to remain in Belgium at liberty to mix with your people and to act and speak for them, there might be great value in the establishment of such a rallying point necessary to the Belgian Nation. But I can hardly hope such would be the outcome of Your Majesty's decision to stay with the Army. It seems to me that Your Majesty must consider the possibility, even probability, of your being taken prisoner, perhaps carried off to Germany, and almost certainly deprived of all communication with the outside world. Such a position would leave your people bereft of their natural leader, without, so far as I can see, any compensating advantage.
>
> (Signed)   GEORGE R. I.

Finally, on the evening of 27 May, after King Leopold had already requested a cease-fire, Churchill dictated the following message to Keyes:

> Belgian Embassy here assumes from King's decision to remain that he regards the war as lost and contemplates separate peace.
> It is in order to dissociate itself from this that the Constitutional Belgian Government has reassembled on foreign soil. Even if present Belgian Army has to lay down its arms, there are 200,000 Belgians of military age in France, and greater resources than Belgium had in 1914 on which to fight back. By present decision the King is dividing the Nation and delivering it into Hitler's protection.
> Please convey these considerations to the King, and impress upon him the disastrous consequences to the Allies and to Belgium of his present choice.

A motor torpedo boat sent over to Nieuport during the night brought Keyes, Davy and other Britons home, but the King and the Queen Mother remained to endure their self-imposed captivity.[23]

Immediately the campaign of vilification began. One of the least plausible charges to be made against King Leopold was that he had failed to give his Allies sufficient advance warning of the impending collapse. Sir Roger Keyes

---

[23] *Keyes Diary* entries for 24-28 May.

and Colonel Davy both kept Lord Gort and the Prime Minister informed day by day of the deteriorating situation on the Belgian front, and Keyes noted that the latter was not surprised when told of the cease-fire. Churchill later wrote that 'the collapse had been foreseen three days earlier'—hence the desperate efforts to persuade the King to escape. Colonel Davy, having motored through the night, saw Pownall at Cassel at about 9.00 am on 27 May and told him that in his opinion the Belgians would have packed up within twenty-four hours. Pownall's indignation is doubly ironic in view of his conviction of the Belgian Army's incompetence throughout the short campaign. If the French Government was not equally well informed the fault lay with their representative at Belgian headquarters, General Champon.[24]

The only point on which the Allies had some small grounds for complaint was the suddenness with which Leopold acted on the afternoon of 27 May when he decided that, from a Belgian viewpoint, his Army and people had suffered enough. Unfortunately Gort and Pownall did not hear of the cease-fire until 11.00 pm, and Blanchard also took several hours to contact. Keyes sent a telegram to Gort at 12.30 pm warning him that a Belgian cease-fire was imminent and shortly afterwards Davy telephoned GHQ, but neither message was received by the C-in-C as Gort was absent from his command post. At 5.00 pm, moreover, Keyes telephoned the Prime Minister from La Panne and asked that the message be repeated to Gort in case the earlier telegram had gone astray. At the same time Davy got through to the War Office but strove in vain to impress the desperate nature of the situation on the Deputy Chief of the Imperial General Staff. Pownall's immediate reaction is significant. 'We heard at Dunkirk that the King of the Belgians had asked for a cease-fire as from midnight. He was bound to, sooner or later, but another twenty-four hours would have made a great deal of difference.' Weygand appears to have had more cause for complaint, though he exaggerated in saying 'We had received no sort of warning. . . so that the news fell on us like a thunderbolt'. General Koeltz, Weygand's representative with the northern armies, visited Belgian headquarters at 3.00 pm on 27 May and noticed the King and Van Overstraeten pacing up and down on the lawn in deep conversation. Koeltz later testified that both Michiels and Van Overstraeten had spoken rudely to him, implying that Belgium had been deserted by her allies. Nothing was said about requesting a cease-fire. According to Overstraeten, the reason Koeltz was not informed was that he (Overstraeten) was still trying to convince the King and Michiels that resistance could be prolonged at least until the next day.[25] Clearly by this time the Belgians were resentful at their allies' failure either to keep them fully informed or to provide more assistance in their final agony. Desperate requests for RAF fighter cover were answered

---

[24] *Ibid.* Churchill p. 83. Cab 65/7 136(40), 23 May. Michiels pp. 210-11. Davy *Unpublished Memoirs.*
[25] *Pownall Diaries* p. 345. J. Weygand pp. 74-5. Shirer p. 848. *Overstraeten* pp. 712-14.

but only a handful of planes succeeded in reaching the front. Accusations were now flying thick and fast between all three allies with only marginal relevance to the actual situation.

Churchill's initial reaction to the sudden Belgian cease-fire was restrained. This was doubtless in part due to the spirited defence of the Belgian war effort presented to the War Cabinet by Keyes and Davy at 11.30 am on 28 May. Davy had been appalled to see a draft communiqué accusing Leopold of treachery and of surrendering without warning. Davy relates how Churchill drafted in his own hand a more moderate communiqué including the phrase 'It is early yet to judge', and then said 'How about that, Colonel Davy?' Davy replied 'That's better, Sir', and the whole room laughed. Keyes' report stressed that the Belgian Government's precipitate flight and the promise of a refuge in France had led to the chaos of refugees which had seriously handicapped the defence; only Leopold's presence had kept the Belgian Army fighting for the last four days. Churchill remarked 'No doubt history would criticize the King for having involved us and the French in Belgium's ruin. But it was not for us to pass judgement on him'.[26] This was, to say the least, a rather selective view of recent Anglo-French-Belgian history.

Unfortunately for King Leopold, he had no equivalents of Keyes and Davy to present his case sympathetically in Paris. On the contrary, at the meeting called by Reynaud at 7.10 pm on 27 May there were present the Belgian Premier, M. Pierlot, and Minister of Defence, General Denis, who both denounced Leopold as a traitor. In fairness to the Belgian ministers, they were under the mistaken impression that the King was negotiating a peace settlement with the Germans and intended to form a new administration. In fact he merely signed an unconditional surrender in his capacity as Commander-in-Chief and became a prisoner of war. In view of Reynaud's own desperate political position it was only too easy to make Leopold the scapegoat for the whole Allied collapse. Immediately after this meeting Reynaud summoned General Spears and the British ambassador, Sir Ronald Campbell, to the Ministry of War. Pétain and Weygand were also present.

> Reynaud was white with rage. 'The King of the Belgians has betrayed us,' he said in a voice of fury. 'Three weeks ago he begged us to fly to his help; today, without a word of warning, he has capitulated.'
> 'There has never been such a betrayal in history,' cried Reynaud. 'To think that this is the man to whose succour we flew is unbelievable. It is monstrous, absolutely monstrous.'
> Weygand, too, was indignant and angry.

Spears's immediate reaction was one of relief that Weygand and Reynaud had responded so vigorously to this latest disaster, but then he noted Pétain's ominous silence and soon after realized that Weygand intended to blame Gort for the Belgian collapse.

[26] Overstraeten pp. 701-2. Davy *Unpublished Memoirs op. cit.*, *Keyes Diary* entry for 28 May. Cab 65/7 144(40), 28 May.

At 8.30 am on 28 May Reynaud made a radio broadcast castigating Leopold III in the bitterest terms for the Belgian surrender, which he described as 'an event without precedent in history'. That evening Reynaud told Spears he was surprised and hurt to find the British Government adopting a very different attitude from his concerning King Leopold. Churchill had told the House of Commons that afternoon that he had no intention at that moment to pass judgement on the King in his capacity as Commander-in-Chief; while in a broadcast Duff Cooper had said: 'The Belgian Army fought bravely, they have suffered heavily, they have yielded only before overwhelming odds. This is no time for criticism or recriminations'. Spears sympathized with Reynaud's view that he needed full British support against the French defeatists and did his best to persuade London to change its tune. Churchill responded in the House of Commons on 4 June 'after a careful examination of the fuller facts then available, and in justice not only to our French Ally but also to the Belgian Government now in London':

> At the last moment when Belgium was already invaded, King Leopold called upon us to come to his aid, and even at the last moment we came. He and his brave, efficient Army, nearly half a million strong, guarded our left flank and thus kept open our only line of retreat to the sea. Suddenly, without prior consultation, with the least possible notice, without the advice of his Ministers and upon his own personal act, he sent a plenipotentiary to the German Command, surrended his Army and exposed our whole flank and means of retreat.

Churchill in his speech, though he omitted the passage from *The Second World War*, went on to refer to the Belgian surrender as 'a pitiful episode' (which) 'compelled the British at the shortest notice to cover a flank to the sea more than 30 miles in length. Otherwise all would have been cut off, and all would have shared the fate to which King Leopold had condemned the finest Army his country had ever formed'. While it is possible to have some sympathy with Churchill's overriding concern to support the French Government in June 1940, it is less easy to accept that he was 'stating the truth in plain terms' in the second volume of *The Second World War* published nine years later.[27]

It is extremely difficult to reach a balanced verdict on King Leopold's policy throughout the campaign of 1939-40 in general and on his termination of hostilities in particular; not least because judgement tends to be influenced by the still controversial history of the King's conduct under German occupation and his eventual abdication. Given two assumptions, however, his policy during the campaign was both consistent and honourable. These are first that as King under the Belgian constitution he had a unique role to play as the actual (not merely nominal) Commander-in-Chief of the Armed Forces, and that as the 'father of his people' (King of the Belgians) his overriding duty was to remain with his troops and people to share their

---

[27] Baudouin p. 60. Spears pp. 245-7, 255. Churchill p. 84. Hansard Parliamentary Debates 5th Series 1939-40 Vol. 361, 28 May (col. 421), 4 June (cols. 788-9).

ordeal and protect them as far as his diminished powers allowed. His ministers continued to believe that once the Army had been compelled to lay down its arms, the King could do more for the future of his country by continuing Belgium's resistance in exile. Whether or not one accepts the wisdom of the King's decision, his motives were entirely honourable in making a choice which he realized would be open to the basest misinterpretation.[28]

The second assumption might be termed a foreign policy of 'limited liability'. Belgium had clung to a policy of strict neutrality from 1936 until actually invaded by Germany in 1940. Before the war Britain and France had accepted this policy but once the war began they urged Belgium to join the alliance.[29] At the Casteau Conference on 12 May, Leopold had accepted co-ordination of his Army by a French general in the Allied interest but he never accepted that the fate of Belgium was indissolubly bound to her temporary allies—in contrast to Churchill's offer of an Anglo-French union. Despite references to the possible evacuation of Belgian troops to continue the struggle overseas it seems clear that for the King the obligation of his Army ended with the defence of the Belgian homeland.

While the King had every right to maintain such a policy of limited liability, it would be unreasonable to expect Belgium's former allies to view it sympathetically between 1940 and 1945. How did Leopold expect the war to terminate when Belgium withdrew from the conflict on 28 May 1940? Certainly he expected France to capitulate within a few days, but what of Britain with whom he had always had more sympathy? At a conference with three of his leading ministers at Wynendaele on 25 May he is reported as having said 'the cause of the Allies is lost . . . No doubt England will continue the War, not on the Continent, but on the seas and in the colonies. But Belgium can play no part in it. Her role is terminated . . . There is no more reason for us to continue the war on the side of the Allies'. This implies that at best Britain would succeed in preserving her own sovereignty. (On 25 May the King told Van Overstraeten that Queen Wilhelmina would be weakening her independence if she remained in Britain. Had he chosen to abandon his Army he would have set up his residence in the Belgian Congo.) Like those Frenchmen who opposed de Gaulle and the Free French, King Leopold apparently did not believe that Britain could eventually, with the help of allies, return to the Continent and liberate Belgium from Nazi tyranny.[30]

---

[28] The abuse which the newspapers of Britain and France in particular heaped upon King Leopold now seems scarcely credible. He was denounced as a coward, traitor or both. It was said, for example, that the Nazis had supplied him with a German mistress. Lloyd George wrote in a Sunday paper on 2 June, 1940: 'You can rummage in vain through the black annals of the most reprobate Kings of the earth to find a blacker and more squalid sample of perfidy and poltroonery than that perpetrated by the King of the Belgians . . . If Belgium ever again tolerates such a monarch, she will share his disgrace'.

[29] Cammaerts prints the Anglo-French Declaration of 24 April 1937 (Cmd 5437), op. cit., pp. 249-50.

[30] Reynaud pp. 420-30. Overstraeten p. 690. Shirer pp. 844-6.

Leopold's subsequent career would probably have been less turbulent had he adopted the more obvious solution of escaping to England at the last moment on 28 May, but he was prevented from doing so by his conception of his duties as Commander-in-Chief and King. He was certainly convinced that he was choosing the harder road.

What should be the verdict on the Belgium Army? Not all the eighteen Belgian divisions reached a high standard of training, equipment and morale and it was unfortunate that the Allies often formed their impression of the Army as a whole from a few inferior reserve units. Nevertheless the Belgian Army probably merited the generous accolade bestowed by the American historian Telford Taylor:

> However history may ultimately judge King Leopold, the verdict on the Belgian Army must certainly be 'well done'. The Belgians were painfully surprised at Eben Emael and the nearby Albert Canal bridges, but the shock gave way not to desperate confusion but to a most determined and well-directed defence. The successive retreats forced upon the Belgians by the French catastrophe were skilfully carried out. The forts and defensive positions were tenaciously held, and the Belgian artillery proved itself exceptionally effective, despite a murderous rain of bombs from a strong enemy... enjoying complete mastery of the skies.
>
> In fact, the Belgians never broke, and Brooke's left flank remained firmly anchored, until the very end, after the Belgians had lengthened and thinned their own front in response to the pleas of the British and French...
>
> For eighteen days Leopold's army held on against the German tide, fighting gallantly long after the course of the larger battle had spelled Belgium's doom. If the quality of the Belgian performance had been duplicated in other lands, the German march of conquest might have been shorter.[31]

Thus ended the darkest day for the Allies since the German breakthrough on the Meuse. The Belgian collapse left a yawning gap from Ypres through Dixmude to the coast which it seemed impossible for the BEF to plug. The western front had also been pierced at several points and the Germans were within artillery range of Dunkirk. Thanks to Weygand's delay in ordering a retreat into the bridgehead around Dunkirk, a large part of I French Army was surrounded south of the Lys. Finally Anglo-French relations were plunging towards their nadir: neither could have received much solace from blaming the Belgians for what seemed certain to be an unmitigated military disaster.

---

[31] Telford Taylor *The March of Conquest* (Hulton, 1959), pp. 251-2.

5

The Miracle of Dunkirk and the Collapse of the Alliance

The nine days (26 May-4 June) during which over 300,000 Allied troops were evacuated from Dunkirk and the neighbouring beaches held widely differing meanings for each of the participants. For the Germans there was something of an anti-climax in the triumphant conclusion of what was, after all, only the first phase in the conquest of Western Europe to be followed, perhaps, by the submission of Great Britain. For Britain the magnitude of the military disaster was mitigated by the unexpected escape of the great majority of her troops and the consoling belief that the RAF and the Royal Navy together constituted an impregnable defence against invasion: there was even a perverse satisfaction at the sloughing off of troublesome allies. For the majority of Frenchmen, on the contrary, Dunkirk spelt the beginning of the end: with her defences turned, the most modernized portion of her armies destroyed, and deserted by her allies, France's capitulation could only be a matter of time.

As for Belgium, although her Government escaped first to France and subsequently to Britain, no organized units were evacuated: 'Dunkirk was an opportunity without significance'.[1]

Dunkirk has been the subject of many detailed studies, not all of them free from nationalistic bias; British writers blaming the French for the ineptitude that made evacuation necessary and the French in turn accusing their ally of desertion at the critical hour. In this chapter no attempt will be made to describe the military operations in detail since that has been ably and sometimes brilliantly done by other historians.[2]

The chapter will concentrate rather on two major historical controversies. First, why the Germans failed to press home the overwhelming advantage they had gained by 22 May by annihilating the Allied armies isolated by the

[1] D. Divine *The Nine Days of Dunkirk* (Faber, 1959), p. 241.
[2] In addition to Divine, for example, see R. Collier *The Sands of Dunkirk* (Collins, 1961); Ellis; and Hervé Cras (Jacques Mordal) *Dunkerque* (Editions France-Empire, 1960).

rapid thrust to the Channel coast. Second, how Anglo-French misunderstanding—and genuine differences in strategy and policy—became so acute during the Dunkirk crisis that the alliance was shattered for all practical purposes.

Although something of a truism, it is sometimes necessary to be reminded that even in the most decisive campaigns the eventual victor as well as the vanquished has his command problems and anxieties. These can easily be glossed over and forgotten in the euphoria of victory, and it is one of the historian's tasks—as happened for example after the Prussian defeat of France in 1870—to show that the winning side was that which made fewer mistakes.

Even while the German armoured divisions were streaking towards the Channel coast some of the senior generals, including Kleist (commanding Rundstedt's Panzer Group) and Kluge (Fourth Army) were anxious about their vulnerable southern flank and favoured putting on the brake.[3] Hitler fully shared their anxiety. As Halder, Chief of the General Staff, noted on 17 May: 'A very disagreeable day! The Führer is excessively nervous. He mistrusts his own success; he's afraid to take risks; he'd really like us to stop now. His excuse is anxiety about our left flank'. The following day, according to Halder, he raved and bellowed and alleged that 'they were well on the way to spoiling the whole operation and even risking the danger of defeat'. Although with every passing day the danger of an Allied counter-attack to isolate the advanced German armour from the mass of infantry diminished, the more cautious German generals grossly exaggerated the threat suggested by the British counter-attack at Arras on 21 May. In particular Kleist, with the approval of Rundstedt and Halder, put restraints on the progress of Guderian's XIX Corps, which had reached Abbeville on 20 May. Guderian had planned to send the 2nd Panzer Division straight on to Boulogne, the 1st to Calais and the 10th to Dunkirk, but he was temporarily deprived of the 10th, while parts of the 1st and 2nd had to be left behind to hold the Somme bridgeheads pending the arrival of motorized infantry. These were but small indications of the harsh brake soon to be applied.

The other major consideration affecting the German command system was the ever-increasing imbalance between Army Groups A and B. In order to exploit Rundstedt's brilliant success on the Meuse and dash towards the Channel, all OKH's reserves were sent to the southern flank and none to Bock. Indeed Army Group B was stripped of all its armoured and motorized troops, much of its tactical air support and even of its infantry reserves. In

---

[3] There is a vast bibliography on the halt order. I have relied chiefly on Telford Taylor *The March of Conquest op. cit.*, 'Dunkirk 1940' by H. A. Jacobsen in Jacobsen and J. Rohwer (eds) *Decisive Battles of World War II: the German View* (Deutsch, 1965). H. A. Jacobsen 'L'Erreur du Commandement Allemand devant Dunkerque' in *Revue Historique de L'armée* No. 3, 1958 pp. 63-74. B. H. Liddell Hart 'The Dunkirk "Halt Order"—a further reassessment' January 1954, (Liddell Hart Archives).

consequence while Army Group B dwindled to twenty-one infantry divisions (some of them dependent on horse transport), by 24 May Army Group A had swollen to over seventy divisions (including all ten Panzer divisions). In short every armoured and motorized unit was crammed into the restricted area between Cambrai, Péronne and the Channel Coast ready to strike against the Allies' southern front from Valenciennes to Gravelines.

Telford Taylor rightly stresses that although the Allies had improvised a continuous defence along the Canal Line and although this was definitely not good tank country, the German superiority in men and weapons was so overwhelming that a determined attack could not long have been withstood.

Despite the restraints already mentioned, Kleist's panzers had begun their north-eastern drive up the Channel coast on 21 May. By 24 May Calais was besieged by 10th Panzer Division while 1st Panzer Division had secured four bridgeheads across the Aa Canal, one of which was barely fifteen miles from Dunkirk.

Meanwhile on the eastern side of the huge pocket Bock had begun a determined attempt to smash through the Belgian defences at two points—north of Ghent and at the junction with the BEF near Audenaarde. Halder was far from pleased by the direction of these attacks because he feared they would only push the Belgians back towards a defensible perimeter on the coast, whereas he had instructed Bock to roll up the Allied line from south to north. Nevertheless, as has been shown, Bock's penetration of the Lys defences on 24 May obliged Gort to rush his reserves to the Ypres area at the very moment when reinforcements were desperately needed on his long western flank and at Calais. For all the gallantry displayed by the defenders of Boulogne, Calais and the Canal line, it is hard to escape the conclusion that there was no military solution to 1st Army Group's problem on the evening of 24 May. Only remarkable blunders on the German side can explain why the total disaster, which even optimists such as Churchill expected, was averted.

The Allies' reprieve resulted from the fact that the German armoured forces were halted along the Canal Line from the evening of 24 to the morning of 27 May. This provided a crucial breathing space which enabled the BEF and part of 1st French Army to withdraw inside the Dunkirk perimeter and prepare to withstand a siege behind the innumerable canals and dykes from Gravelines through Bergues to Nieuport. Not surprisingly the origins and purposes of this 'halt order' became one of the most controversial questions in the history of the Second World War. There is now a reasonable consensus of opinion among historians but the subject can still produce heated argument.

The German halt order stemmed from two connected problems: first the need to co-ordinate Army Groups A and B as the corridor separating them shrunk and to give one of them the predominant role in the final phase; and second, the need to rest and regroup before driving across the Somme.

On the evening of 23 May General Brauchitsch gave the surprising order

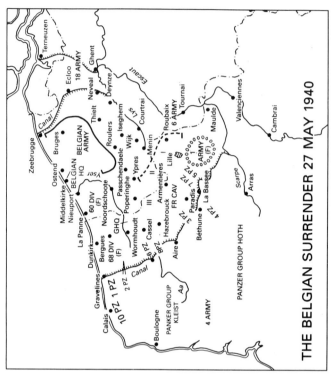

THE BELGIAN SURRENDER 27 MAY 1940

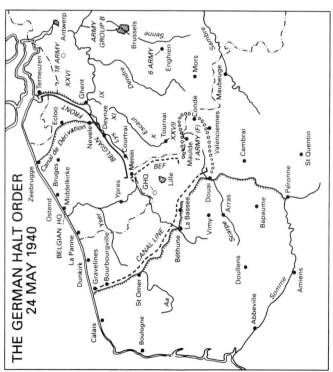

THE GERMAN HALT ORDER 24 MAY 1940

that Bock's Army Group B would have the honour of applying the *coup de grace*; Kluge's Fourth Army would be transferred to Bock's command from 8.00 pm on 24th. Halder concluded that Brauchitsch was evading his own responsibility and he withheld his signature to signify his disapproval of the order. Simultaneously, in response to a plea from Kluge, Rundstedt issued instructions for a momentary halt on the morrow (24 May) to allow the bulk of the infantry units to close up. This has sometimes been wrongly taken as the origin of the halt order which Hitler merely confirmed.[4] In fact it was not a binding order and was not interpreted as such by the field commanders. Guderian's and Reinhardt's Panzer Corps both resumed their advance early on 24 May and made bridgeheads across the Canal Line at Bourbourgville and St Omer respectively.

The origins of the halt order are more correctly attributable to the meeting of Rundstedt and Hitler at the former's headquarters at Charleville in mid-morning on 24 May. Hitler not merely agreed that the armour should be halted on the Canal Line but emphatically stated that it should be conserved for the coming offensive south of the Somme. The Führer also said that if the ring encircling the enemy was compressed too tightly it would restrict the activities of the Luftwaffe. That evening Hitler interviewed Brauchitsch at Supreme Headquarters, cancelled the transfer of Fourth Army to Bock and instructed OKH to issue an order establishing the Canal Line as the limit of the armoured advance. Thus although Hitler was almost certainly influenced by Rundstedt's cautious attitude it was he who issued the halt order despite the strong objections of Brauchitsch.

Hitler saw the Commander-in-Chief again the following morning and Halder's record revealed that political considerations played a decisive role in the former's thinking. Hitler wished the battle of annihilation to be fought on French rather than Flemish soil. Consequently he cast Bock's Army Group in the totally unsuitable role of hammer with Rundstedt's Group as the anvil. High hopes were also pinned on the Luftwaffe. 'This divergence of view', Halder concluded wearily, 'results in a tug of war which costs more nerves than does the actual conduct of operations. However, the battle will be won, this way or that'. Moreover Hitler disrupted the orthodox chain of command by delegating responsibility to Rundstedt to decide whether the advance should be resumed. The latter, who was still worrying about the need for motorized infantry to close up behind the armour, consequently disregarded with impunity an OKH instruction to resume the attack. Army Group A's War Diary for 25 May concludes with the complacent observation that 'The task of the army group can be considered to be in the main completed'. It is safe to deduce that Rundstedt was now preoccupied with

---

[4] CF Ellis pp. 138-9, 150-1, 347-53 who is inaccurate in a number of details.

the second phase and had no desire to see his armoured forces squandered among the dykes and canals around Dunkirk.[5]

Halder and Brauchitsch continued to fret at what they regarded as a nonsensical military decision; namely a halt on the virtually open western side and a frontal assault by comparatively weak forces against a well-organized eastern front which was systematically being withdrawn. By midday on 26 May Hitler was converted to this viewpoint as a result of Bock's slow progress and the failure of the Allies to try to break out westward.[6] He ordered the armoured divisions to renew their advance towards Dunkirk and Cassel. Fortunately for the Allies this order took about sixteen hours to implement; some of the units were resting or engaged in repairs and maintenance work, and new orders had to be drafted. Momentum had been lost and was never to be recovered against stubborn defence of the perimeter. By 28 May Guderian acknowledged this by requesting that his armoured divisions be withdrawn to rest and refit.[7]

Thus, in ascending order of importance, Goering, Rundstedt and Hitler all shared responsibility for the German halt order. Goering's vanity seems to have driven him to a rash promise which the Luftwaffe could not fulfil—as it would do again with even worse consequences at Stalingrad. Rundstedt's motives are apparent in his whole conduct of the campaign. On the one hand he took a rather cautious view of mechanized warfare, being acutely sensitive about his vulnerable southern flank and the high rate of wastage of his tanks. His senior subordinates, Kleist and Kluge, also urged a pause to allow the infantry to close up. All were aware moreover that the Dunkirk area was difficult for tanks, though it must be stressed that had Guderian been allowed to press on unchecked in the first place he would have encountered far weaker opposition than after the halt. On the other hand Rundstedt was not particularly concerned about mopping up the surrounded allies; this unpleasant business could be left to Bock's infantry while his armour prepared for the great offensive across the Somme. Hitler's motives were complex. He had displayed great anxiety, almost panic, during the advance and fully endorsed Rundstedt's caution. It is also reasonable to speculate that he preferred to see Goering and the Luftwaffe rather than the generals reap the final honours in clinching the victory. Goering certainly put this point to Hitler in a telephone conversation on 23 May. Hitler was furious with OKH and even suspected Brauchitsch of disloyalty over the attempted transfer of Fourth Army.

Few historians now accept the view that Hitler's behaviour was influenced

---

[5] Telford Taylor *op. cit.*, p. 261: 'it is as absurd to contend (as do the German generals in their postwar apologia) that Rundstedt had no responsibility for the stop-order as to argue (as does Major Ellis) that Rundstedt had already acted on May 23 and that Hitler merely "endorsed" Rundstedt's decision.'

[6] By the morning of 26 May, Kluge, Kleist and even Rundstedt were coming round to the view that the halt order would have to be lifted.

[7] Ellis pp. 158-9 lays insufficient stress on the lapse of five days between Guderian's initial desire to press on to Dunkirk and his decision on 28 May that tanks would be largely ineffective.

by the desire to let the British off lightly in the hope that they would then accept a compromise peace. True, in his political testament dated 26 February 1945 Hitler lamented that Churchill was 'quite unable to appreciate the sporting spirit' in which he had refrained from annilating the BEF at Dunkirk, but this hardly squares with the contemporary record. Directive No. 13, issued by Supreme Headquarters on 24 May called specifically for the annihilation of French, English and Belgian forces in the pocket, while the Luftwaffe was ordered to prevent the escape of the English forces across the Channel. Moreover 'an annihilating reprisal' was demanded for English attacks on the Ruhr, and the struggle against the English homeland was to be continued, including unrestricted naval warfare.[8]

However, beyond all these particular considerations, the overriding factor seems to have been that the German leaders simply could not believe that a large-scale evacuation from Dunkirk was possible. Since Churchill himself thought the British would be lucky to rescue even 45,000 men, while the French were reluctant to embark any of their troops until 29 May, this explanation does not appear so fanciful. Nevertheless a great opportunity was missed. The halt order would never have been issued had Hitler and his senior generals grasped the urgency of cutting the Allies off from the sole remaining port before the Royal Navy could be organized for 'a huge salvage operation'.

Apart from the errors of judgement already mentioned, the German High Command was slow to take action on the obvious problem that as the Allied pocket became ever more constricted so a plethora of higher headquarters would attempt to direct fewer and fewer divisions actually operating against the perimeter. In fact the chain of command became hopelessly confused. On 30 May the operations officer of 4 Army complained that 'nothing is going on today, (that) no one is now interested in Dunkirk'. In fact it was only on that day that OKH realized the magnitude of the Allies' evacuation effort. Halder glumly noted that bad weather had grounded the Luftwaffe 'and now we must stand by and watch countless thousands of the enemy get away to England right under our noses'. At last the command structure was simplified by delegating to Kuechler's 18th Army, with only ten divisions operating on the perimeter, full responsibility for finishing off the battle. This was a very unsuccessful day for the German forces surrounding Dunkirk nor, despite attacks all along the perimeter on the next day (31 May), was a break-in achieved. Indeed 31 May was the best day for the defenders with about 68,000 troops evacuated to England. By the morning of 1 June the total number evacuated was approaching 200,000. Thanks primarily to the halt order it was already possible to speak of 'the miracle' of Dunkirk.

By 30 May the bulk of 1st Army Group, except for the Belgian Army and

[8] *The Testament of Adolf Hitler* (Icon Books, 1962), entry for 26 February 1945. H. R. Trevor-Roper (ed) *Hitler's War Directives 1939-1945* (Sidgwick and Jackson, 1964), pp. 28-9.

some 50,000 French troops surrounded in the Lille pocket, had successfully withdrawn inside the Dunkirk perimeter. Lord Gort and his commanders had by now no doubt that their primary task was to save as much of the BEF as possible; indeed Gort himself reluctantly obeyed Churchill's order to return home on the night of 31 May. Unfortunately the French commanders within the perimeter had received less clear cut orders and were in addition far less well prepared for evacuation. Consequently no unified command ever functioned inside the perimeter, and to the French the escape of the BEF looked far less 'heroic' than when viewed from across the Channel. 'The British Lion', Admiral Darlan wrote scornfully to his wife, 'seems to grow wings when it's a matter of getting back to the sea'.

On 27 May three French naval staff officers visited Dover and were fully briefed on Admiral Ramsay's preparations for evacuation which had been in progress for over a week. After the war General Weygand expressed amazement at the extent of British naval preparations, yet he and Reynaud had been informed of the British Government's decision to evacuate on the previous day, and no attempt had been made to conceal preparations from the French. More significantly, Admiral Darlan had initially argued that evacuation was impossible and as late as 30 May Spears recorded his (Darlan's) opinion that Dunkirk might hold out easily for eight days because its heavy naval guns could fire inland. He refused to elaborate. Even on the afternoon of 31 May Admiral Abrial, nominally commanding the bridgehead, told General Alexander that he had no thought of evacuation of troops other than non-combatant specialists.[9]

At the same time some of the French leaders, especially Weygand, were making accusations of disloyalty combined with exorbitant demands of the British. Until Churchill's speech in the House of Commons on 4 June Reynaud repeatedly made bitter references to the British failure to underwrite his charges against King Leopold, whom the French clearly wished to cast in the role of scapegoat. Another embarrassing demand was that British troops evacuated from Dunkirk should immediately be shipped back to the Somme front. Spears vainly pointed out that although his Government intended to send more organized reinforcements to France (and of course did so) it could not be expected to sacrifice exhausted and weaponless men to no purpose. He was irritated to learn later that French troops evacuated from Dunkirk would rest for at least a month.

In no respect did the French plead more urgently for assurances of all-out British support than in the air, but the latter were increasingly hardening in the view that, except over Dunkirk, the remainder of Fighter Command must be reserved for the impending battle of Britain. Spears discovered on 29 May that the French had all but replaced the 520 aircraft they had lost

---

[9] Spears p. 278. Weygand *Recalled to Service* pp. 86-7. Nigel Nicolson *Alexander: the Life of Field-Marshal Alexander of Tunis* (Weidenfeld and Nicolson, 1973), pp. 104-5.

during the campaign and that losses in personnel amounted to only 350. The RAF had even less admiration for General Vuillemin and the French Air Force than Gort and his commanders had for the French High Command. Lastly, Reynaud uttered dark threats to Spears about the attitude of French public opinion unless French troops were evacuated in equal numbers with the BEF.[10]

Churchill now called upon all those qualities that made him an incomparable war leader, including courage, vision, generosity and rhetoric, in an attempt to cement the crumbling alliance. Baudouin and Spears have left brilliant eye-witness descriptions of his confrontation with the French leaders at a Supreme War Council held at the Ministry of War in Paris on 31 May.[11]

Churchill attempted to open the meeting on a cheerful note. The evacuation from Dunkirk, he remarked, was proceeding with unhoped-for success: up to noon that day 165,000 men had been rescued. Weygand interrupted in a high, querulous and aggressive voice 'But how many French? The French are being left behind'. Spears' description of Churchill's reaction deserves to be quoted at length:

> The Prime Minister looked at him for a moment. The light had died out of his face, his fingers were playing a tune on the edge of the table; out came his lower lip as if he were going to retort, and I expected one of those sentences that hit like a blow, but his expression changed again, it was evident that he felt every indulgence must be shown to people so highly tried, undergoing so fearful an ordeal. He looked very sad, and as he spoke a wave of deep emotion swept from his heart to his eyes, where tears appeared not for the only time that afternoon. 'We are companions in misfortune,' he said, 'there is nothing to be gained from recrimination over our common miseries.'
>
> The note he had struck was so true, went so deep, that a stillness fell over the room, something different from silence, it was like the hush that falls on men at the opening of a great national pageant. I imagine all thoughts were turned inwards, questioning whether each one was observing the precept. It was important in its results, for the note it struck was maintained through the meeting; goodwill, courtesy and mutual generosity prevailed.

Churchill explained that there were two main reasons why only 15,000 of the total so far evacuated were French: there had been many British administrative units near the coast who had been taken off before any fighting troops; and, more important, the French had so far received no clear orders to evacuate. Henceforth evacuation would proceed on equal terms—'Bras dessus bras dessous'. With tears in his eyes Churchill told the French that his Government had taken the harsh decision to leave the wounded behind in order to save more fighting men.[12]

Reynaud exploited Churchill's praise of the superiority of British fighter aircraft (which were said to be exacting German losses at the rate of four or five to one) by requesting that, as soon as the Dunkirk operation was over,

[10] Spears pp. 263-96 *passim*.
[11] *Ibid* pp. 288-309, Baudouin pp. 70-3.
[12] Spears pp. 288-9, Churchill pp. 97-8.

the full strength of the RAF should be deployed to protect the French front on the rivers Somme and Aisne. He was sure Germany would not attack Britain until France was completely defeated. Churchill would not be drawn to give a rash promise beyond undertaking that an advance air striking force at Le Mans consisting of six bomber and three fighter squadrons would be kept in being and its losses made good. He had to point out that although the RAF pilots had proved their individual superiority, the Germans possessed a numerical advantage of at least two and a half to one. It was one thing to operate from British bases over Dunkirk but the fighters' range would limit their usefulness over the Somme. He then stated the viewpoint of the Air Staff and the Chief of Fighter Command, Air Marshal Dowding, which remained constant for the rest of the campaign:

> I told you a fortnight ago, when we threw in those squadrons, that this was our last reserve. That was the truth. We had 39 fighter squadrons allocated to the defence of Great Britain. We gave you 10 of these to be employed for three or four days of your most critical fighting only. I do not know where they are now. I think very little of these 10 squadrons remains. Great Britain is left with only 29 squadrons to meet a concentrated attack, on the most dangerous targets of all, the factories producing new aircraft. The factories are our greatest danger.

Reynaud gratefully acknowledged the magnificent support of the RAF and particularly the recent dispatch of 10 squadrons from Britain's slender reserve, but the French were not satisfied. The Prime Minister, spurred on by Weygand, returned to the charge the following day and Spears was obliged to point out that 'you cannot suddenly improvise air bases and whisk over ground staffs and all the paraphernalia they need'. Reynaud was not mollified, observing 'Your people do not seem to realize their fate is in the balance; they are acting as if they were merely interested onlookers'. Baudouin drew the conclusion that the British were already coolly assuming that the French would succumb: 'England', he wrote, 'has already put on mourning for us'.[13]

Among the many inter-Allied problems discussed at the Supreme War Council none would arouse the French to more bitter recrimination than those of the command of the bridgehead, parity in evacuation and the provision of a rearguard.

Early in the meeting Churchill gave a masterly analysis of the situation at Dunkirk. The garrison at present comprised General Fagalde's two excellent though weakened divisions (60th and 68th), de la Laurencie's two very reduced divisions and three British divisions. Churchill magnanimously

[13] Baudouin pp. 71-3. Spears pp. 297-9, 318-9. When the German attack started on 10 May the RAF had in France a total of ninety-six fighters, 160 light bombers and 160 other aircraft. During the battle an additional ten fighter squadrons and many replacements were sent out. The RAF lost 959 aircraft, of which 477 were fighters, and 1,192 personnel in the Battle of France—Spears p. 299.

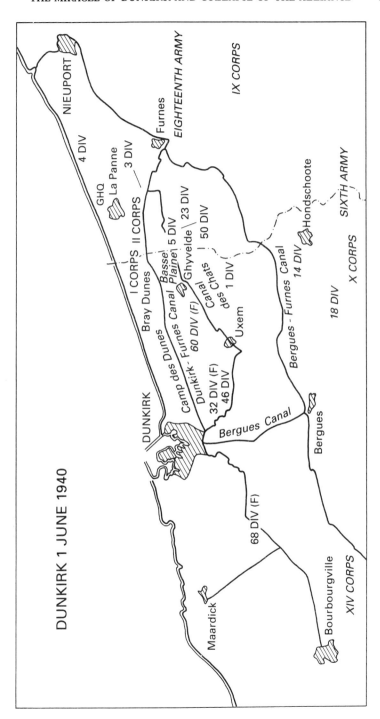

DUNKIRK 1 JUNE 1940

proposed that the British would stand firm and allow the French to escape. They would do this in honour; it would be their contribution to comradeship. During the discussion Admiral Darlan proposed that a telegram embodying their decisions so far should be sent at once to Abrial. Churchill erupted when the third draft paragraph was read out stating that when the units defending the bridgehead embarked the British would go first (Reynaud relates that he anticipated Churchill's reaction so that the phrase had probably been inserted deliberately). 'Certainly not', Churchill boomed, 'the three British divisions will form the rearguard. As so few French have got out so far, I will not accept further sacrifices by the French'. Spears admits that for the first time he felt out of sympathy with the Prime Minister's strong and generous emotion:

> His emotions were leading him too far, I thought, he was being too generous. After all, if we were in such dire jeopardy, it was due to colossal French incompetence and, steeped as I was in the French atmosphere, I knew that in French eyes we only came into the picture in so far as we could help France. Perfectly natural perhaps, but we, on the other hand, ought not to sacrifice our chance of survival to the French, who certainly would not do so for us.

The final draft of the telegram stated merely that 'the British troops will remain behind us as long as possible', but it was hardly surprising if the Frenchmen present later recalled Churchill's repeated offer to provide a rearguard. As for a unified command, when Reynaud proposed that Abrial should command the whole evacuation Sir John Dill, the CIGS, objected on the grounds that communications were too difficult; matters must be left to the commanders on the spot. Gort himself had been ordered to embark that night and the British hoped that Blanchard might be given similar instructions. The British clearly had no confidence in the French commanders. Nevertheless the British raised no objections to the final text of the telegram to Abrial, which read as follows:

> 1. The Bridgehead will be held round Dunkirk with the divisions under your command and those under British command, for the purpose of enabling Allied troops to embark.
> 2. As soon as you are convinced that no troops outside the Bridgehead can make their way to the points of embarkation, the troops holding the Bridgehead will withdraw and embark, *the British forces acting as a rearguard as long as possible.*
> 3. Once Dunkirk has been completely evacuated of land and naval units, the harbour will be blocked. The British Admiralty will be responsible for this operation, subject to due notice being given to it in good time by you.
> 4. The evacuation at Dunkirk will be carried out *under your orders.* (My emphasis.)[14]

The divergent policies pursued by the two allies and the absence of a unified command rendered what in any case would have been a near-chaotic situation even uglier. The French troops were embittered by the BEF's

---

[14] Spears pp. 293-5, 301-2, 308. Baudouin p. 72. Reynaud *In the Thick of the Fight* p. 451.

ruthless abandonment of weapons and equipment which the former thought should have been used to hold the bridgehead. There was a real danger that the Allies would come to blows. There were instances when British and French columns drove through each other's lines only by threatening force. Here are two instances related by Captain D. Barlone, a pro-British officer of the Second North African Division:

> May 29, 1940, 'a fresh traffic block, a mile long ... where the British have barricaded all exits so that their columns can pass through with greater ease. The French are wild. Some gunners talk of training their guns on them and shooting. As the senior officer present I take command and order two artillery officers to take a hundred men and drag away the heavy British tractors which bar the road. Then I go out and find an English major, and in five minutes everything is arranged...' And again, May 31, 1940: 'In the dim light of dawn, we can see the British embarking from a wooden wharf, on the other side of the dock, for we each have our own quay-side in order to avoid confusion and friction'.

Until 29 May the French had no orders to embark and Gort, seeing no French vessels, at first refused to permit French soldiers to be taken aboard British ships. Even after he had received orders to embark an equal number of Frenchmen it proved impossible to do so.

Although on the whole discipline was remarkably well preserved, some officers as well as troops put their own safety first. Major Miles Reid, a liaison officer with 1st Army, saw French and Belgian officers driving onto the beaches assigned to British embarkation, refusing to turn back when ordered and disabling their cars so as to prevent their enforced removal. A French general and his aide-de-camp were manhandled by British troops when they attempted to force their way on board a ship for which they had no permit. Even General Alexander, a paragon of cool efficiency under pressure, confessed privately that he was shocked by incidents of British indiscipline—particularly the rushing of already packed boats—which he witnessed.[15]

While the Supreme War Council was meeting in Paris there occurred yet another Allied misunderstanding such as had characterized the whole campaign. This incident, involving command of the bridgehead and arrangements for the final stages of the evacuation, had particularly serious repercussions on Anglo-French relations. It remains a matter of historical controversy.[16]

Admiral Abrial had been under the impression, certainly since the Cassel Conference on 27 May, that Weygand had placed him in command of Dunkirk and its immediate vicinity. This impression was strengthened when Gort visited his headquarters at his subterranean command post on the morning of 31 May to announce his departure the same evening and the transfer of authority to General Alexander. Precisely what Gort said to Abrial

---

[15] In this section I have drawn heavily on John C. Cairns 'Great Britain and the Fall of France' op. cit., pp. 374-5. See also N. Nicolson, Alexander p. 111. Miles Reid, Last on the List (Leo Cooper, 1974), pp. 56-7.

[16] The main sources used in the following paragraphs are: N. Nicolson, Mordal, Chapman, Ellis, W. G. F. Jackson Alexander as Military Commander (Batsford, 1971), and Gort's Second Despatch.

is hard to discover but, according to the former's Dispatch he informed Alexander that he was to operate under the orders of Abrial—though with the traditional right of appeal to the British Government, and to assist the French in the defence of Dunkirk. At the same time he was to occupy himself with arrangements for the evacuation of his troops, while making sure that the French shared equally in the evacuation facilities. The final paragraph read significantly:

> If at any time in your judgement no further organized evacuation is possible, and no further proportionate damage can be inflicted on the enemy you are authorized in consultation with the Admiral du Nord to capitulate formally to avoid useless slaughter.[17]

In order to understand the unenviable situation in which Alexander now found himself a word needs to be said about the circumstances of his appointment. Gort held a final conference with his Corps commanders at La Panne at 6.00 pm on 30 May to which Alexander, still commanding 1st Division, was not invited. The Commander-in-Chief probably expected that a large part of I Corps would have to capitulate and he selected Lieutenant General M. G. H. Barker to command the rearguard. According to Field Marshal Montgomery it was he who persuaded Gort to change his mind and appoint the far abler Alexander. Actually Gort did not need advice either on Alexander's abilities or Barker's shortcomings, but whether or not Montgomery's intervention was decisive is not of great importance. What matters is that Alexander missed the final conference and only heard of his appointment on the morning of 31 May. He took the precaution of telephoning the War Office and was told that his duty was to hold the Dunkirk perimeter for as long as possible, provided the safety of the BEF was not imperilled. Unfortunately the two parts of this instruction soon appeared to Alexander to be incompatible.

When Alexander went to see Abrial on the afternoon of 31 May he had no idea of the 'appalling commitments' which Churchill was just then undertaking on his behalf in Paris. Nor had he much confidence in the French admiral, who was attempting to command the perimeter from an underground casemate, bastion 32. Even before meeting Abrial, Alexander must have been in some doubt about his priorities: he had been placed under French command and yet both Gort and the War Office had stressed the importance of evacuating his troops as rapidly as possible. Captain W. G. Tennant, a British naval officer who accompanied Alexander to bastion 32, recalled hearing Gort tell the latter that he was to do nothing to imperil his army.

The British general and the French admiral at once found themselves at cross purposes. The latter proposed to reduce the bridgehead still further and to hold a front on an intermediate line east of Dunkirk running from Bergues

[17] Ellis p. 234.

through Uxem and Ghyvelde to Basse Plaine. According to Alexander's Brigadier General Staff, William Morgan, who was present, Abrial still had no thought of a general evacuation but only of specialists. Alexander declared the proposed withdrawal to be impracticable: if the bridgehead were to be further contracted the enemy's close-range artillery fire would make continued evacuation impossible. In any case he did not expect the perimeter to hold for more than another 36 hours. He added that the British troops were absolutely exhausted and that he intended to withdraw from the present perimeter at midnight.

In short Alexander decided to exercise his right of appeal to the British Government at the very first orders he received, while Abrial in turn appealed to Weygand. Although Alexander did not contact the War Office until 8.15 pm that evening, Eden had evidently not yet heard of Churchill's chivalrous undertaking in Paris that the British would provide the rearguard. The Secretary of State consequently accepted Alexander's account of the imminent collapse of the bridgehead and ordered him to withdraw his force as rapidly as possible on a fifty-fifty basis with the French (ie, equal numbers to be embarked from now on), aiming at completion by the night of 1-2 June.

At least Alexander now had unambiguous orders but he realized that Abrial had been led (by either Gort or Weygand or both) to expect a very different role from the last British divisions. On the return journey to Abrial, Alexander told Brigadier Morgan that he had never been in a worse position and he wished he had been hit by a shell.

According to the French historian Benoist-Méchin, Abrial had now received the telegram conveying the decisions of the Supreme War Council, including confirmation of his own authority and Churchill's undertaking to provide the rearguard. Alexander could only refer to his recent conversation with Eden, but he did make a concession by agreeing to maintain the existing eastern defences for a further twenty-four hours, ie, until midnight on 1 June. Thus, as the British Official Historian points out, although Alexander proved wrong in believing the intermediate line could not be held (it was in fact gallantly held by the French for two days after the British had left), he did hold the forward position on the Bergues-Furnes Canal for a further twenty-four hours whereas Abrial had proposed its prompt abandonment.[18]

By midnight on 1 June the British had withdrawn through the intermediate line (Uxem-Ghyvelde) now manned by the French; the Germans did not follow up in the darkness and by dawn on 2 June all but about 4,000 of the BEF had embarked. This remnant dispersed among the dunes and the outskirts of Dunkirk to await evacuation the following night. This could hardly be termed a rearguard; indeed Alexander reported that apart from shelling and bombing the troops were not interfered with. Three miles to the

[18] This account generally follows N. Nicolson, *Alexander*, pp. 100-114, Ellis pp. 239-40 and Cairns p. 376.

east the Germans fiercely attacked the French line all day but failed to break through. It was an ironic situation. If Churchill had had his way the rearguard would have been entirely British; Gort had expected the final honour and sacrifice to be shared; in the event the rearguard was entirely French.

Many Frenchmen at the time and since have regarded Alexander's withdrawal and embarkation as tantamount to desertion. Jacques Mordal, for example, wrote that the British were determined to pull out at all costs with no thought of the stragglers from 1st French Army who were still trickling in. Sir William Jackson in his recent study *Alexander as Military Commander* also reaches a remarkably severe verdict: 'A true ally would have stayed, but British commanders reflect their country's view and will always place the safety of their troops above considerations of an alliance. Mistrust of foreigners runs deep and inevitably comes to the surface in times of crisis'. This comes close to admitting the charge which Blanchard, Weygand and others had been levelling against their ally throughout the campaign. Is the accusation just?

Alexander was certainly mistaken in his belief on 31 May that the intermediate line could not be held and that the bridgehead itself would shortly be overrun. In extenuation it may be said that he greatly underestimated the number of French troops within the perimeter, but it seems more pertinent to say that he underestimated the determination and staying power of Fagalde's units, half of them composed of elderly reservists. From this miscalculation sprang his decision to evacuate the BEF as quickly as possible while taking an equal number of Frenchmen if practicable. However I Division's War Diary for the night of 2 June records 'there was to be no embarkation by the French until the British were finished'.[19]

What does seem to be clear is that by this stage Britain's military leaders, including the War Office, had lost confidence in the French High Command and were beginning to think increasingly of salvaging as much as possible from the Continental disaster in preparation for the defence of the homeland. Churchill's heroic gesture in offering to provide the rearguard was out of key with this disillusioned attitude, but he was soon to show himself equally resolute on the issue of air support to France. It would be unjust, however, to place much responsibility for the misunderstanding at Dunkirk on Alexander's shoulders. He appears to have received ambiguous orders from Gort at the last minute and was certainly unaware of Churchill's proposals in Paris until after he had received War Office approval to evacuate his troops. On his return to England, Churchill endorsed Alexander's interpretation of the situation in a message to Weygand.

> Enemy closing in on reduced bridgehead. By trying to hold on till to-morrow we may lose all. By going to-night much may certainly be saved, though much will be lost. Nothing like numbers of effective French troops you mentioned believed in bridgehead now, and we doubt whether such large numbers remain in area. Situation cannot be fully judged by

[19] N. Nicolson, *op. cit.*, pp. 112-13. Chapman pp. 227-9.

Admiral Abrial in the fortress, nor by you, nor by us here. We have therefore ordered General Alexander, commanding British sector of bridgehead, to judge, in consultation with Admiral Abrial, whether to try to stay over tomorrow or not. Trust you will agree.

Alexander's professional reputation in Britain was, if anything, enhanced by his conduct at Dunkirk.[20]

Even in French eyes, Britain emerged more favourably from the Dunkirk operation, thanks mainly to the Royal Navy, than had seemed possible on 29 May. On that day Captain Tennant had reported to the Admiralty 'The French staff at Dunkirk feel strongly that they are defending Dunkirk for us to evacuate—which is largely true'. But from 29 May to the end the British exactly achieved the goal of equal evacuation—139,732 English to 139,097 French. Even more impressive, between 31 May and the morning of 3 June 20,000 British troops were evacuated (ie, all that remained) as against 98,000 French. Yet more Frenchmen could have been embarked had they been organized at the right place and the right time. Tragically, several British ships sailed with spare room on the night of 2/3 June leaving thousands of Frenchmen behind. That night, before leaving, Alexander toured the beaches east of the Dunkirk mole in a small boat vainly trying to find more troops, French or British to take off.

The Admiralty, however, made one more heroic attempt on the night of 3/4 June and took off over 26,000 Frenchmen to make a total of about 53,000 since the last British troops had left—a gesture of comradeship which was widely recognized by French writers. Between 30 and 40,000 French troops remained to be taken prisoner on 4 June including, unfortunately, several thousands of the gallant rearguard. According to Admiralty records the grand total of British and Allied troops landed in England during Operation Dynamo was 338,226. A few thousand more sailed directly to French ports.[21]

For France of course the conclusion of the Dunkirk evacuation signified no crowning mercy of deliverance as it did for Britain. It marked but a further step towards the catastrophic defeat which very few thought could be averted. Gratitude, particularly warmly expressed by Reynaud, for the gallant efforts of the Royal Navy, was speedily submerged by the bitter recrimination at the British Government's stubborn refusal to sacrifice the RAF in the battle of France which began on 5 June. General Vuillemin had demanded as a minimum the despatch of half Britain's fighter force (at least 20 squadrons) to French bases. The British Government's conclusion that

---

[20] Churchill pp. 100-101. In addition to Alexander, the generals whose reputations were most enhanced by the campaign were Brooke and Montgomery. Lord Gort suffered the usual fate of British Commanders-in-Chief at the outset of a great war and was not given another field command; but his Chief of Staff, Lieutenant General Sir Henry Pownall, retained Churchill's confidence and received a succession of important appointments including VCIGS (1941), C-in-C Far East (1941-2) and Chief of Staff South-East Asia Command (1943-4).

[21] *Ibid* p. 102, for a table of numbers evacuated day by day. See also Ellis pp. 247-8 and D. Divine pp. 252-4. For losses of men and equipment during the campaign see Divine pp. 264-5 and Spears p. 351.

this would be an unjustifiable gamble was strengthened by reports from Spears and others that the French were making very poor use of their own air forces, even in comparison with the small British contingent still operating on French soil.

Churchill's stiff reply provoked an hysterical anti-British outburst from Weygand in the French War Committee on 6 June. He resurrected the old charge that Gort had refused to attack at Arras and declared himself wholly in support of Vuillemin.

> . . . Mr Churchill may think General Vuillemin's demands unreasonable. Perhaps if he saw the condition of our Army he would think that we were unreasonable to go on fighting. He would not countenance the RAF choosing its own targets when it was supposedly under him as commander-in-chief. If the British were sincere, they would place the whole RAF under Vuillemin. He demanded that all fighters be sent to France. And when Spears very tartly suggested that the French air force could have no idea of the useful work done by the British because no French pilots were in the skies to observe, the general blew up. 'Here are the English,' he shouted, 'dictating to us who their Commanders are to be. The French are masters in their own house.'

Five days later when Churchill confronted Weygand in person he made the British position absolutely clear. 'Here is the decisive point', Weygand declared, pleading for all out British aid, 'Now is the decisive moment'. The Prime Minister was adamant. 'This is not the decisive point', he remarked, 'and this is not the decisive moment'. That moment would come, everyone present understood, when Hitler unleashed his forces against Britain.[22]

Dunkirk, as John Cairns has aptly written, marked 'the nadir of Anglo-French military relations'. Despite Churchill's brave and repeated attempts to keep the political alliance afloat it seemed clear to the French, even to Reynaud, that after Dunkirk Britain was preoccupied with ensuring her own salvation. The frenetic appeals mingled with virulent accusations that flowed from Weygand and others only served to underline their realization that the alliance had disintegrated beyond repair. Churchill's most famous speech, uttered in the House of Commons on the afternoon of 4 June, only rubbed the point in.

'WE SHALL FIGHT ON THE BEACHES, WE SHALL FIGHT ON THE LANDING-GROUNDS, WE SHALL FIGHT IN THE FIELDS AND IN THE STREETS, WE SHALL FIGHT IN THE HILLS; WE SHALL NEVER SURRENDER. . .'[23]

His rhetoric implied all too clearly that the French would surrender.

The breakdown of the alliance was sensitively recorded and brilliantly

---

[22] Cairns p. 379. Spears pp. 353, 360. Colonel H. Redman, General Ismay's senior representative in France informed Spears on 4 June that on an urgent request a few days previously the twenty-seven RAF fighters in service in France had flown 127 sorties in one day. The French had over 300 fighters available that day but only achieved eighty sorties.

[23] Churchill p. 104.

described by Spears, who dined that night with French friends in whose company he had hitherto felt in complete communion with France.

> But that night there was a rift between us, a slight crack in the crystal cup sufficient to change its sound when touched. I had my password and they did not have theirs. We no longer belonged to one society bounded by the same horizon. A lifetime steeped in French feeling, sentiment and affection was falling from me. England alone counted now.

Spears, like so many Britons, felt a curious sense of relief when Dunkirk was over; indeed he experienced a renewed sense of confidence that this marked the beginning for Britain. Despite the temporary destruction of the BEF, Eden at home confessed to similar optimism. When the King asked why he seemed in wonderful spirits, he replied: 'Now we are all alone, Sir. We haven't an ally left'.[24] Indeed George VI wrote to his mother, 'Personally I feel happier now that we have no allies to be polite to and pamper'; while Beaverbrook declared, on returning from the final Supreme War Council in France, 'We're all Splendid Isolationists now'.[25] Is it to be wondered at that few Frenchmen could sympathize with this strange brand of insular arrogance or complacency which, for reasons beyond the imagination of most men in June 1940, proved in the long run to be absolutely justified?

[24] Spears p. 361. Eden p. 113.
[25] Sir John Wheeler-Bennett *George VI* (Macmillan, 1958), p. 460. A. J. P. Taylor *Beaverbrook* (Hamish Hamilton, 1972), p. 437.

APPENDIX

Chief Dramatis Personae
1939-1940

Belgium

PIERLOT, HUBERT — Prime Minister since 1937.

SPAAK, PAUL-HENRI — Foreign Minister since 1936.

DENIS, GENERAL HENRI — Defence Minister since 1936.

OVERSTRAETEN, GENERAL RAOUL VAN — Aide-de-camp and military adviser to King Leopold.

BERGEN, GENERAL EDOUARD VAN DEN — Army Chief of Staff since 1936. Dismissed in January 1940 for removing barriers on French frontier.

MICHIELS, GENERAL OSCAR — Succeeded van den Bergen as Chief of Staff.

DELVOIE, GENERAL MAURICE — Military Attaché in Paris.

France

DALADIER, EDOUARD — Prime Minister and Minister of National Defence 1938-March 1940, Minister of National Defence 20 March-18 May 1940; and Foreign Affairs 18 May-June 1940.

REYNAUD, PAUL — Finance Minister 1938-March 1940. Prime Minister March-June 1940.

BAUDOUIN, PAUL — Under-Secretary of State in Reynaud's Government. Enjoyed considerable power due to his influence over Reynaud's mistress, Mme de Portes.

PÉTAIN, MARSHAL HENRI PHILIPPE — Retired in 1930 aged 75. War Minister 1934. Ambassador in Spain 1939-40, Deputy Prime Minister 18 May-16 June 1940. Prime Minister of Vichy régime 1940-1944.

GAMELIN, MAURICE — Commander-in-Chief of the Armed Forces and Chief of Staff 1935-19 May 1940. Supreme Commander of the Allied Armies in France 1939-1940.

WEYGAND, MAXIME — Commander-in-Chief 1931-1935 and 19 May-22 June 1940.

DARLAN, ADMIRAL JEAN — Commander-in-Chief French Navy.

VUILLEMIN, GENERAL JOSEPH — Commander-in-Chief French Air Force.

GEORGES, GENERAL ALPHONSE — Commander, North-East Front.

BILLOTTE, GENERAL G. H. G. — Commander 1st Army Group (under Georges). Co-ordinator of Allied Armies in North Eastern France and Belgium from 12 May 1940. Fatally injured in a car crash on 21 May.

BESSON, GENERAL A. M. B. — Commander 3rd Army Group (from 22 May).

BLANCHARD, GENERAL J. M. G. — Commander 1st Army. Succeeded Billotte 24 May-1 June.

PRIOUX, GENERAL R. J. A. — Commander 1st Army's Cavalry Corps. Succeeded Blanchard 24 May. Taken prisoner 29 May.

GIRAUD, GENERAL H. H. — Commander 7th Army. 18 May 1940 transferred to 9th Army but taken prisoner on 19 May.

FRÈRE, GENERAL AUBERT — Succeeded Giraud in command of 7th Army.

DE LA LAURENCIE, GENERAL FOURNEL — Commander III Army Corps.

ALTMAYER, GENERAL RENÉ — Commander V Army Corps. Evacuated to England on 31 May.

Germany

BRAUCHITSCH, GENERAL WALTHER VON — Commander-in-Chief of the Army, 1938-1941.

HALDER, GENERAL FRANZ — Chief of Staff of the Army, 1938-1942.

BOCK, GENERAL FEDOR VON — Commander of Army Group B.

REICHENAU, GENERAL WALTHER VON — Commander 6th Army in Army Group B.

KUECHLER, GENERAL GEORG VON — Commander 18th Army in Army Group B.

RUNDSTEDT, GENERAL GERD VON — Commander Army Group A.

KLUGE, GENERAL GUENTHER VON — Commander 4th Army in Army Group A.

KLEIST, GENERAL EWALD VON — Commander Panzer Group in Army Group A.

GUDERIAN, GENERAL HEINZ — Commander XIX Panzer Corps in Kleist's Group.

ROMMEL, GENERAL ERWIN — Commander 7 Panzer Division in General Hoth's VI Panzer Corps.

Great Britain

CHAMBERLAIN, NEVILLE — Prime Minister May 1937-10 May 1940.

CHURCHILL, WINSTON S. — First Lord of the Admiralty September 1939-10 May 1940. Prime Minister and Minister of Defence May 1940-1945.

HORE-BELISHA, LESLIE — Secretary of State for War May 1937-January 1940.

EDEN, ANTHONY — Secretary of State for War May-December 1940.

GORT, GENERAL LORD

Chief of the Imperial General Staff 1937-September 1939, Commander-in-Chief BEF 1939-1940.

IRONSIDE, GENERAL SIR EDMUND

Inspector-General Overseas Forces May-August 1939. CIGS, September 1939-27 May 1940.

POWNALL,
LIEUTENANT GENERAL SIR HENRY

Director of Military Operations, War Office 1938-39. Chief of the General Staff BEF 1939-40.

DILL, LIEUTENANT GENERAL
SIR JOHN

Commander I Corps BEF 1939-April 1940. VCIGS April-May 1940. CIGS 27 May 1940-November 1941.

BROOKE,
LIEUTENANT GENERAL SIR ALAN

Commander II Corps BEF.

ADAM, LIEUTENANT GENERAL
SIR RONALD

Commander III Corps BEF.

ALEXANDER, MAJOR GENERAL
THE HON. HAROLD

Commander 1 Division BEF. Commander of Rearguard (I Corps) at Dunkirk 31 May-4 June 1940.

British Allied Missions, 1939-1940

HOWARD-VYSE,
    MAJOR GENERAL SIR RICHARD

General Ironside's representative with the French High Command (Gamelin's Headquarters).

SWAYNE, MAJOR GENERAL
    SIR JOHN

Lord Gort's representative at French GQG (Georges' headquarters).

SPEARS,
    MAJOR GENERAL SIR EDWARD

Prime Minister's Personal Representative with the French Prime Minister May-June 1940.

REDMAN,
    LIEUTENANT COLONEL HAROLD

Head of a small detachment of the Military Section of the War Cabinet Secretariat, sent to form a direct link with the French organization that most nearly corresponded—the Secretariat du Conseil Supérieur de la Défence Nationale. In practice the French Secretariat was not much used so that Colonel Redman's mission had to link up more directly with Gamelin's staff at Vinçennes.

KEYES, ADMIRAL SIR ROGER

Special liaison officer from the War Cabinet to King Leopold of the Belgians 1939-1940.

NEEDHAM,
    MAJOR GENERAL HENRY

Head of the War Office Mission to Belgian GHQ May 1940. Injured in a motor accident and succeeded by Lieutenant Colonel George Davy on 17 May.

BIBLIOGRAPHY

Public Record Office

The principal classes of Cabinet Papers consulted for this study were as follows:

Cab 23—   Cabinet Minutes.
Cab 2—   Comittee of Imperial Defence Minutes.
Cab 65/1-13 War Cabinet Conclusions and Confidential Annexes, September 1939-June 1940.
Cab 66/1-8   War Cabinet Memoranda, September 1939-June 1940.
Cab 53   Chiefs of Staff Committee Minutes (1923-1939).
Cab 79/1-4   Chiefs of Staff Committee Minutes, September 1939-June 1940.
Cab 80/1-11 Chiefs of Staff Committee Memoranda, September 1939-May 1940.

Private Papers

ARCHDALE, Lieutenant-Colonel A. O.: *Notes on Liaison, October 1939-May 1940* (Mrs A. O. Archdale).

DAVY, Brigadier G. M. O.: Unpublished *Memoirs* and other Papers relating to Anglo-Belgian Liaison in May 1940. (Brigadier G. M. O. Davy).

KEYES, Admiral Sir Roger: Papers relating to his visits to Belgium in 1939-1940 (Churchill College, Cambridge).

MACLEOD, Colonel R. E.: Papers relating to the career of Field Marshal Lord Ironside. (Colonel R. E. Macleod).

POWNALL, Lieutenant General Sir Henry: *Diaries, 1933-1944.* (Liddell Hart Centre for Military Archives, King's College, London).

Select Bibliography

BANKWITZ, P. C. F.   *Maxime Weygand and Civil-Military Relations in Modern France.* (Cambridge, Mass: Harvard U.P., 1967).

BARLONE, D.   *A French Officer's Diary* (Cambridge University Press, 1942).

BARNETT, Correlli, BOND, Brian et al.   *Old Battles and New Defences* (Brassey's, 1986).

BAUDOUIN, P.   *The Private Diaries of Paul Baudouin* (Eyre & Spottiswoode, 1948).

BAUER, E.   *La Guerre des Blindés* Vol I (Lausanne: Payot, 1962).

BEAUFRE, A.   *1940: the Fall of France* (Cassell, 1967).

BÉDARIDA, F.   *La Stratégie Secrete de la Drôle De Guerre* (Presses de la Fondation Nationale Des Sciences Politiques, 1979).

BELL, P.M.H.   *A Certain Eventuality: Britain and the Fall of France* (Saxon House, 1974).

BENOIST-MÉCHIN, J.   *Sixty Days that Shook the West* (Cape, 1963).

BLOCH, Marc   *Strange Defeat* (New York, Norton Library, 1968).

BOND, Brian   *British Military Policy between the Two World Wars* (Oxford University Press, 1980).

BOND, Brian (ed)   *Chief of Staff: the Diaries of Lieutenant General Sir Henry Pownall Vol I 1933-1940* (Leo Cooper, 1973).

BRYANT, A.   *The Turn of the Tide, 1939-1943* (Collins, 1957).

BURDICK, C. & JACOBSEN, H-A.   *The Halder War Diary, 1939-1942* (Greenhill Books, 1988).

BUTLER, J. R. M.   *History of the Second World War. Grand Strategy Vol II* (H.M.S.O., 1957).

CAMMAERTS, E.   *Belgium: the official account of what happened, 1939-1940* (Evans, nd).

CHAPMAN, Guy	*Why France Collapsed* (Cassell, 1968).
CHURCHILL, W. S.	*The Second World War Vol II* (Cassell, 1949).
COLVILLE, J. R.	*Man of Valour. Field Marshal Lord Gort V.C.* (Collins, 1972).
DENNIS, Peter	*Decision by Default* (Routledge, 1972).
DILKS, David (ed)	*The Diaries of Sir Alexander Cadogan, 1938-1945* (Cassell, 1971).
DIVINE, David	*The Nine Days of Dunkirk* (Faber, 1959).
DOUGHTY, Robert A.	*The Seeds of Disaster: the Development of French Army Doctrine, 1919-1939* (Hamden Ct: Archon Books, 1985).
DUROSELLE, J-B.	*Politique Étrangère de la France: L'Abîme 1939-1945* (Paris: Imprimerie Nationale, 1983).
EDEN, A. (The Earl of Avon)	*The Eden Memoirs: Vol II The Reckoning* (Cassell, 1965).
ELLIS, L. F.	*History of the Second World War: The War in France and Flanders 1939-1940* (H.M.S.O. 1953).
FRASER, D.	*Alanbrooke* (Collins, 1982).
GAMELIN, M.	*Servir* 3 Vols (Paris: Plon, 1946).
GATES, Eleanor M.	*End of the Affair: the Collapse of the Anglo-French Alliance, 1939-1940* (Allen & Unwin, 1981).
GILBERT, M.	*Finest Hour: Winston S. Churchill 1939-1941* (Heinemann, 1983).
GOUTARD, A.	*1940: La Guerre des occasions perdues* (Paris: Hachette, 1956).
GUNSBURG, J. A.	*Divided and Conquered: The French High Command and the Defeat of the West, 1940* (Greenwood Press, 1979).
HALPERN, P. (ed)	*The Keyes Papers* Vol III (Allen & Unwin, 1981).
HAMILTON, N.	*Monty: The Making of a General 1887-1942* (Hamish Hamilton, 1981).
HARVEY, J. (ed)	*The Diplomatic Diaries of Oliver Harvey, 1937-1940* (Collins, 1970).
HORNE, A.	*To Lose a Battle: France 1940* (Macmillan, 1969).
HOWARD, M. E.	*The Continental Commitment* (Temple Smith, 1972).
JACKSON, W. G. F.	*Alexander of Tunis* (Batsford, 1971).

JACOBSEN, H-A. &   *Decisive Battles of World War II: the German*
ROHWER, J. (eds)   *View* (Deutsch, 1965).

KEMP, A.   *The Maginot Line: Myth and Reality* (New
York: Military Heritage Press, 1988).

KENNEDY, J.   *The Business of War* (Hutchinson, 1957).

KEYES, R.   *Outrageous Fortune: the Tragedy of Leopold
(Lord Keyes)   III of the Belgians, 1901-1941* (Secker &
Warburg, 1984).

KIEFT, D. O.   *Belgium's Return to Neutrality* (O.U.P., 1972).

Le GOYET, P.   *Le Mystère Gamelin* (Paris: Presses de la
Cité, 1975).

*Les Relations Militaires Franco-Belges, Mars
1936-10 Mai 1940* (Paris: Centre Nationale
de la Recherche Scientifique, 1968).

LIDDELL HART, B.   *History of the Second World War* (Cassell,
1970).

LYET, P.   *La Bataille de la France Mai-Juin 1940*
(Paris: Payot, 1947).

MACLEOD, R. &   *The Ironside Diaries 1937-1940* (Constable,
KELLY, D. (eds)   1962).

MANSTEIN, E. von   *Lost Victories* (Methuen, 1958).

MEARSHEIMER, J. J.   *Conventional Deterrence* (Ithaca, New York:
Cornell University Press, 1984).

MICHEL, H.   *La Drôle de Guerre* (Paris: Hachette, 1972).

*Le Defaite de la France, Septembre 1939-Juin
1940* (Paris: Presses Universitaires de
France, 1980).

MICHIELS, O.   *18 jours de guerre en Belgique* (Paris: Berger-
Levrault, 1947).

MINNEY, R. J.   *The Private Papers of Hore-Belisha* (Collins,
1960).

MONTGOMERY, Viscount   *The Memoirs of Field Marshal Montgomery*
(Collins, Fontana 1961).

MORDAL, J.   *Dunkerque* (Paris: France-Empire, 1960).

MURRAY, Williamson   *The Change in the European Balance of Power
1938-1939* (Princeton N.J.: Princeton
University Press, 1984).

NEAVE, A.   *The Flames of Calais* (Hodder & Stoughton,
1972).

NICOLSON, N.   *Alex: the Life of Field Marshal Alexander of
Tunis* (Weidenfeld & Nicolson, 1973).

PAILLAT, C.   *Dossiers Secrets de la France Contemporaine*

Vol 4 *La Guerre Immobile Avril 1939-10 Mai 1940* and Vol 5 *La Guerre Éclair 10 Mai 1940-24 Juin 1940* (Paris, Robert Laffont 1984 and 1985).

PRIOUX, A.   *Souvenirs de Guerre 1939-1945* (Paris, Flammarion, 1947).

REYNAUD, P.   *Au Coeur de la Melée* (Paris, Flammarion, 1951 and English edition *In the Thick of the Fight* (Cassell, 1955).

ROTON, G.   *Années Cruciales, 1933-1940* (Paris: Charles Lavauzelle, 1947).

SHIRER, W. L.   *The Collapse of the Third Republic* (Pan Books, 1972).

SLESSOR, J.   *The Central Blue* (Cassell, 1956).

SPEARS, E. L.   *Assignment to Catastrophe* (2 Vols Heinemann, 1954 Reprint Society one volume ed, 1956).

STENGERS, J.   *Leopold III et le gouvernement: les deux politiques belges de 1940* (Paris-Gembloux: Duculot, 1980).

TAYLOR, T.   *The March of Conquest: The German Victories in Western Europe, 1940* (New York: Simon & Schuster, 1967).

THOMPSON, L.   *1940: Year of Legend, Year of History* Collins, 1966).

TREVOR-ROPER, H. R. (ed)   *Hitler's War Directives* (Sidgwick & Jackson, 1964).

VAN OVERSTRAETEN, R.   *Albert I-Leopold III: vingt ans de politique militaire belge, 1920-1940* (Brussels: de Brouwer, n.d.).

VANWELKENHUYZEN, J.   *Neutralité Armée: La Politique Militaire de la Belgique pendant la Drôle de Guerre* (Brussels: La Renaissance du Livre, 1979).

Les Avertisssements Qui Venaient de Berlin Octobre 1939-Mai 1940 (Paris: Editions Duculot, 1983).

VILLELUME, P. de   *Journal d'Une Défaite, Août 1939-Juin 1940* (Paris, Fayard, 1976).

WARLIMONT, W.   *Inside Hitler's Headquarters* (Weidenfeld & Nicolson, 1964).

WEYGAND, M.   *Recalled to Service* (Heinemann, 1952).

WOLFERS, A.   *Britain and France between Two Wars* (New York: Norton Library, 1966).

YOUNG, R. J.
In Command of France: Foreign Policy and French Military Planning, 1933-1940 (Cambridge Mass: Harvard University Press, 1978).

Articles

ALEXANDER, Donald W.
'Repercussions of the Breda Variant'.
(*French Historical Studies*, Spring, 1974).

ALEXANDER, Martin S.
'Prophet without Honour? The French High Command and Pierre Taittinger's Report on the Ardennes Defences, 1940'.
(*War and Society*, May 1986).

ALEXANDER, Martin S.
'La Grand Bretagne, La Belgique et le "Cas Hollande" Décembre 1938-Février 1939'
(*Centre de Recherches et d'Études Historiques de la Seconde Guerre Mondiale* No 7, April 1982).

CAILLOUX, R.
'Campagne de France 1940: la contre attaque qui n'eut jamais lieu 19-25 Mai'.
(*Revue Historique de l'Armée*, No 3 1966).
'1939-1940: la Guerre en France et dans les Flandres vue par les Anglais'
(*Revue Historique de L'Armée*, No 1 1958).

CAIRNS, John C.
'Great Britain and the Fall of France: a Study in Allied Disunity'.
(*Journal of Modern History*, December 1955).
'Along the Road back to France'.
(*American Historical Review*, April 1959).
'"A Nation of Shopkeepers" in Search of a Suitable France'.
(*American Historical Review*, June 1974).
'Some Recent Historians and the "Strange Defeat" of 1940'.
(*Journal of Modern History*, March 1974).

DAVIDSON, Major General F. H. N. 'My Mission to Belgium, 1940'. (*Royal United Services Institute Journal*, December 1969).

DHERS, P. 'Le Comité de Guerre de 25 Mai 1940'. (*Revue d'Histoire de la Deuxième Guerre Mondiale*, June 1953).

HAWES, Major General L. A. 'The Story of the "W Plan"'. The Move of our Forces to France in 1939'. (*Army Quarterly*, July 1971).

JACOBSEN, H-A. 'L'Erreur du Commandement Allemand devant Dunkerque'. (*Revue Historique de L'Armée*, No 3 1958).

PARKER, R. A. C. 'Britain, France and Scandinavia, 1939-1949'. (*History*, October 1976).

SAUNDERS, M. G. 'L 'Evacuation par Dunkerque'. (*Revue d'Histoire de la Deuxième Guerre Mondiale*, June 1953).

STOLFI, R. H. S. 'Equipment for Victory in France in 1940'. (*History*, February 1970).

TRYTHALL, A. J. 'The Downfall of Leslie Hore-Belisha'. (*Journal of Contemporary History*, Vol 16 1981).

VANWELKENHUYZEN, J. 'L'alerte du 10 Janvier 1940'. (*Revue d'Historique de la Deuxième Guerre Mondiale*, October 1953).
'Leopold III et ses ministres, L'Entreveue du 20 Mai 1940 ou La Double Méprise'. (*Centre de Recherche et d'Études Historiques de la Seconde Guerre Mondiale* No 13, 1987).

VIAL, J. 'Une semaine décisive sur la Somme, 18-25 Mai 1940'. (*Revue Historique de l'Armée*, December 1949 and March 1950).

WANTY, E. 'Improvisation de la liaison belgo-britannique du 10 au 18 Mai 1940'. (*Revue d'Histoire de la Deuxième Guerre Mondiale*, January 1964).
'La Défense des Ardennes en 1940'. (*Revue d'Histoire de la Deuxième Guerre Mondiale*, January, 1964).

YOUNG, R. J. 'The Aftermath of Munich: the Course of

French Diplomacy, October 1938 to March 1939'.
(*French Historical Studies*, Vol III Fall, 1973).
'Preparations for Defeat: French War Doctrine in the Inter-War Period'.
(*Journal of European Studies*, June 1972).

Index